D0626832

Praise for
360° Life and Billy Joe Daugherty

"The life, witness, character, and ministry of Billy Joe Daugherty are a light and extend a quality of leadership that will continue to influence the church everywhere. *360° Life* is a special gift at this moment, so soon after his home-going to eternal glory. But it is preceded, and will long be exceeded, by the harvest his ministry will continue to garner though the sowing of his life and teaching. My respect for Billy Joe in every regard was and remains as high as I have felt for any leader I have known through my fifty-plus years as a pastor and friend to the body of Christ. His consistency at every pivotal point of life—as a believer in Jesus, a disciple under His lordship, and as a servant to His church—underwrites the credibility and worth of what each reader will find in this book."

>—JACK W. HAYFORD, founding pastor of The Church
>On The Way and chancellor of The King's College
>and Seminary

"In *360° Life,* Billy Joe Daugherty extrapolates the essence of faith, ushering in a hope that overcomes life's greatest challenges. He masterfully leads us back to the resurrection power of Christ that breaks us free from the fears of our past to live a victorious life."

>—T. D. JAKES, pastor of The Potter's House

"Pastor Billy Joe Daugherty had a profound influence on my life. There are few men who exemplified such integrity and character as Billy Joe. He loved well his wife, family, and the church they both founded. He lived the life he preached and honored God in all he did. In light of this, it's fitting that his final book should be called *360° Life,* because he truly lived this book. Even after his passing, Billy Joe's life continues to multiply. Everything he did was motivated by his desire to build lives and the kingdom of God. This book has the potential to radically transform and infuse your life with faith and a new level of trust in God."

—JOHN BEVERE, international speaker, best-selling
author, and founder of Messenger International

"*360° Life* is a legacy piece from a friend and mentor who always made faith the practical solution to whatever you faced."

—RON LUCE, president and founder of Teen
Mania Ministries

From the Foreword

"Billy Joe Daugherty was a great man of God…a man of integrity and honesty, and he deeply cared about people…. I think when Billy Joe got to heaven, he was greeted first by the Lord Jesus Christ who said, 'Very well done, my good and faithful servant,' and then Billy Joe was greeted by all the ones he won to Jesus from around the world who had gone home before him."

—DODIE OSTEEN, co-founder of Lakewood Church
in Houston

Ten Ways You Can Live
More Richly, Deeply, Fully

BILLY JOE
DAUGHERTY

WATERBROOK
PRESS

360° LIFE
PUBLISHED BY WATERBROOK PRESS
12265 Oracle Boulevard, Suite 200
Colorado Springs, Colorado 80921

The stories in *360° Life* come from real people. Their words have been edited for style and length but not content.

ISBN 978-0-307-45932-9
ISBN 978-0-307-45933-6 (electronic)

Library of Congress Cataloging-in-Publication Data
Daugherty, Billy Joe.
   360° life : ten ways you can live more richly, deeply, fully / Billy Joe Daugherty. — 1st ed.
       p. cm.
   Includes bibliographical references and index.
   ISBN 978-0-307-45932-9 (alk. paper) — ISBN 978-0-307-45933-6 (electronic : alk. paper)
   1. Christian life. I. Title. II. Title: 360 degree life.
   BV4501.3.D374 2010
   248.4—dc22

                                          2010001926

Printed in the United States of America
2010—First Edition

10 9 8 7 6 5 4 3 2 1

SPECIAL SALES
Most WaterBrook Multnomah books are available at special quantity discounts when purchased in bulk by corporations, organizations, and special-interest groups. Custom imprinting or excerpting can also be done to fit special needs. For information, please e-mail SpecialMarkets@WaterBrookMultnomah.com or call 1-800-603-7051.

○ ○ ○

This book is dedicated to the memory and honor of my beloved husband,
Pastor Billy Joe Daugherty,
a great leader among leaders in his community
and in the body of Christ throughout the world.

He truly understood and lived a life of faith
in Jesus Christ from every angle.

My life and the lives of our family, friends, ministry staff,
and congregation will never be the same because of knowing him.

—Sharon Daugherty

Contents

Acknowledgments

I would like to express my gratitude to WaterBrook Press / Random House and to senior editor Bruce Nygren, who edited the chapters of this book.

I would also like to thank…

Tom Newman, a close ministry friend and executive producer of 360life.tv, who invested an enormous amount of time and work in this book throughout the entire project.

Marilyn Price, who has been my husband's personal editor through the years.

Florence Wells, my husband's executive assistant for the past seventeen years.

Finally, I would like to acknowledge the spiritual mentors who have impacted both my husband's life and my life over the years.

—Sharon Daugherty

Note from the Publisher

Sadly, on November 22, 2009, during the process of writing this significant book, author Billy Joe Daugherty passed away. It is both ironic and notable that at the time of his death, the work that Billy Joe was writing was titled *360° Life*. It is fitting that his legacy includes this call to live out the full and vibrant life God intends for each and every one of us.

The writing of the manuscript was almost complete at the time of Pastor Daugherty's untimely death. With the assistance of Sharon Daugherty, Larry Walker, and Tom Newman, final touches were applied and the book was finished.

We are particularly grateful to Sharon Daugherty (with assistance from others in the Daugherty family) for her willingness to write an epilogue to this work. Her insights on Billy Joe's life and ministry—as well as the role of *360° Life*—provide a meaningful overview of her husband's passionate faith. It helps make this book an enduring tribute to one of God's mighty saints.

We offer our prayers to Billy Joe's family, his church, and the many, many people he touched in life. Although Billy Joe Daugherty is now among the great cloud of witnesses in heaven, we trust that through this publication his words will continue to touch people's hearts for years to come.

Foreword by Dodie Osteen

Billy Joe Daugherty was a great man of God and a friend of my family for years. He was lovable, kind, compassionate, merciful, and, in fact, walked like Jesus did. He was a man of integrity and honesty, and he deeply cared about people.

You can look at his family and see that his children have the same traits and characteristics of their father. That means he not only cared about his sheep (people all around the world who he ministered to), but he loved, cared about, and spent time with his family. He loved them as our heavenly Father loves us. They are all in the ministry now because their father was the same at home as he was in the pulpit. Billy Joe and Sharon were so proud of their four children.

Billy Joe was a man of many titles. He labored long and hard at whatever God led him to do. Not only did he pastor a great church, but he also started the Victory World Missions Training Center and the Tulsa Dream Center. Hundreds of missionaries were supported by Billy Joe, and they are prospering and carrying on because this pastor had a love and calling to do what he did for them. They will be forever grateful to this man—and so is Jesus!

All five of my children attended Oral Roberts University, and Billy Joe Daugherty made a lasting impression on them. One of my daughters taught at Victory Christian School and loved it. I know that all the students were grateful that their parents chose Victory Christian School for them to attend.

The Bible says we won't stumble if we walk in integrity. Billy Joe walked in integrity, and God helped him in all that he did. His precious mother told me that Billy Joe was a great football player. He was good in all sports, except he was not a really fast runner in track. She related the story about the time he was running and saw someone running behind him. When he looked back, he saw his dad. I know for a fact that even though Billy Joe has left us for his eternal reward, he is running in the spirit with Sharon, the children, and the work, not only in Tulsa, but all around the world.

I think when Billy Joe got to heaven, he was greeted first by the Lord Jesus Christ who said, "Very well done, my good and faithful servant," and then Billy Joe was greeted by all the ones he won to Jesus from around the world who had gone home before him.

I salute Billy Joe Daugherty and his remarkable family. I am so glad they have been a part of my life. I hold them all in high esteem and honor.

—Dodie Osteen
Co-Founder of Lakewood Church, Houston

1

Resurrection

What if you only had a few days to live?
Would you love?
Would you laugh?
Would you give?
Would you live differently from the way you do
right now?

Now **imagine** for a moment that you are...*dead.*
(Because eventually, it's gonna happen.)

But then one day someone (Jesus) gives you
a second chance at life.
A resurrection.
A fresh start.
A clean slate.
A do-over.

Would you be happier?
Would you be more compassionate?
Would you laugh more?
Would you give more?
Would you forgive more?

Now **imagine** what would happen...
to your hopes
to your dreams
to your marriage
to your relationships
to your family
...if you lived every day like **Resurrection day.**

This thing called the Resurrection changed everything! Everyone who witnessed the execution of Jesus Christ thought it was over when He was nailed to a Roman cross and brutally crucified.

The great man was suddenly a dead man.

His friends wiped away their tears and buried Jesus in a borrowed stone tomb. His enemies were excited—and suspicious. They pressed the Roman governor until he posted a squad of Roman soldiers at the sealed tomb. They didn't want any monkey business.

Their problem was larger than monkeys, however: they were trying to interfere with God's plan. From the beginning of time, He had intended for humankind—His highest creation—to experience a wonder-filled life: a life spent with Him, a life that was free of disease, hatred, anger, violence, hunger, and loneliness.

From their beginning at Creation, Adam and Eve enjoyed that blessed life, but they lost it when they disobeyed God's warnings and chose their own way in the Garden of Eden. (See the Bible account in Genesis 3.)

That first sin of rejecting God's way tainted our entire human race with sin and death—we all have inherited their defective DNA of the soul. This spiritual disease called sin was passed from one generation to the next, with a death sentence that was unavoidable.

The result wasn't God's intention. It was humankind's choice.

But God loved us so much that He gave His innocent Son, His only Son, to save us. Jesus shed His blood and washed away our sins and failures through the wounds He experienced on the cross and in the savage beating by temple guards and Roman soldiers lashing away with their bone-and-stone-embedded scourges.

He died in your place. He paid for your sins. If you receive Him, He declares you, "Not guilty!" He justified you just as if you had never sinned. This is the mercy and grace of God.

Everyone, friend and enemy alike, thought it was over after the followers of the Carpenter placed His battered body in that cold stone tomb. Few remembered and no one believed that Jesus would rise from the grave on the third day.

He knew it, believed it, and willingly laid down His life in full confidence that His Father was able and committed to raise Him from death. The Bible says the Spirit of God entered His dead body and raised Him from death (see Romans 8:11).

WE ALL FEAR DEATH

The Resurrection is important because we all fear death. We work hard to mask it, reframe it, or pretend otherwise. Yet death is a hot topic in our culture. It dominates our television dramas, novels, TV and Internet news, and blog sites. We watch and read about death by war, disease, murder, and natural disaster—as told by victims, survivors, crime-scene investigators, and the mourners left behind. We are fascinated by death. We just don't want it to visit our house.

A dark fear lurks inside the human heart, framed in the burning question: "What will happen to me when I die?"

I have good news on this topic! God broke the power of death on the third day when He raised Jesus from the grave! He stripped Satan of the power he had gained through Adam's sin. And that was when Jesus, fresh from His resurrection, said, "All authority has been given to Me in heaven and on earth" (Matthew 28:18, NASB).

Jesus regained what Adam had lost. He paid the ultimate price—His life—to purchase eternal life for you and me. His resurrection from the dead declared He was the only Son of God. He is alive forevermore!

Now do you see why the Resurrection is so important?

That same Spirit that raised Christ from the dead can come to live inside of you! You can be transformed and born again from the inside out. The old you will pass away, and you will be a new creation in Christ Jesus (see 2 Corinthians 5:17).

This is how you become a child of God! And this is why the fear of death should have no power over you! With Christ as your Savior, when your body is finally laid to rest, your spirit—the real you—will slip out of your body and remain alive forever with God.

If you put your hand in a glove, that glove moves when you move. Once you pull your hand out of the glove, it lies motionless and empty. Your hand represents your "spirit man," and your body is your "earth glove." When the earth glove wears out, the same power that raised Christ from the dead also removes your spirit man from the empty body—and your life continues.

That is the power of the Resurrection! Now you can live without the fear of death and fully enjoy life! Because He lives, you can live—with joy, peace, and right standing with God. Fear will release its grip on your life.

"O Death, where is your sting? O Hades, where is your victory?… But thanks be to God, who gives us the victory through our Lord Jesus Christ" (1 Corinthians 15:55, 57).

During His stay on earth, Jesus showed that He had power over death. The report of one incident reveals His love and compassion toward those dealing with the painful reality of death:

> And behold, there came a man named Jairus, and he was a ruler of the synagogue. And he fell down at Jesus' feet and begged Him to come to his house, for he had an only daughter about twelve years of age, and she was dying.
>
> But as He went, the multitudes thronged Him.…
>
> While He was still speaking, someone came from the ruler of the synagogue's house, saying to him, "Your daughter is dead. Do not trouble the Teacher."
>
> But when Jesus heard it, He answered him, saying, "Do not be afraid; only believe, and she will be made well." When He came into the house, He permitted no one to go in except Peter, James, and John, and the father and mother of the girl. Now all wept and mourned for her; but He said, "Do not weep; she is not dead, but sleeping." And they ridiculed Him, knowing that she was dead.
>
> But He put them all outside, took her by the hand and called, saying, "Little girl, arise." Then her spirit returned, and she arose immediately. (Luke 8:41–42, 49–55)

But the power Jesus displayed over death did not disappear when He ascended to heaven. Just ask Heather.

Clinically Dead, Supernaturally Raised!

THE HEATHER ROSS STORY

The family doctor thought he had a simple case with an obvious treatment when seventeen-year-old Heather came to his office.

Heather's mother had brought her in the moment she realized Heather's symptoms were worse than usual. The doctor decided she had strep throat. "The doctor prescribed penicillin—even though everyone else in my family was very allergic to it. I told him I'd never taken the antibiotic before, but he wasn't worried about it."

The doctor wasn't worried, so Heather didn't worry either. Once she took the penicillin, things took a sudden turn… "I got really ill and laid down. When I woke up, I felt like I needed to vomit so I started to get up, but I could barely stand.

"When I started down the hall to the bathroom (about twenty feet), I was so unsteady that my head was bouncing against both walls. I finally made it, but as I began to vomit I passed out and everything lodged into my throat while I was unconscious."

The normal flow of oxygen to Heather's brain had been interrupted. She was dying minute by minute. She passed out around 11:30 that morning, after her mother had gone to work. Her mother returned from work just after 4:30 p.m. and discovered Heather sprawled on the floor. Five long hours had gone by.

> "**O**h, God, just get me through this. Just give
> me one more chance, just one more day!"

Panic hit because Heather was a type 1 diabetic. Her mother feared that Heather's blood sugar levels had dropped to dangerous levels. When none of the usual procedures she did seemed to work, Heather's mother called the paramedics.

Once the doctors at the hospital completed their initial examination, they came out with some shocking news: Heather was clinically brain dead. (Her mother remembers the doctors saying, "She is a vegetable.") No one knew at the time that Heather was much more aware of her surroundings than anyone suspected. Heather said, "I could hear people around me talking! I remember the nurse who told my aunt and uncle, 'You know, she's pretty much gone.'

"During that time, God asked me, *What are you doing for Me? What are you doing with your life? What is the purpose of your life?* And I didn't have any answers.

"I was a typical teenager who thought, *Hey, I'm seventeen. I'll do whatever I want. After all, it doesn't affect anyone else!* But now in my heart I was crying out, *Oh, God, just get me through this. Just give me one more chance, just one more day!*"

Heather's mother finally left the hospital room to pray. In the middle of her tears and brokenhearted pleas, God spoke to her heart: *You can give up, or you can fight. It's up to you.* She knew the answer. "Okay, I'm gonna fight for this!" She renewed her battle for the life of her child and began to pour out her heart in urgent prayer and determined intercession in the name of Jesus.

"For the first time in two and a half days, I opened my eyes. And within a week I was out of the hospital, walking and talking! I was just as good as I was before I got sick, only twelve times better!

"Once you die and come back to life again, you have a new realization of what true life can be. I am living proof of God's hope and healing." (Adapted from videotaped interview.)

○ ○ ○ ○ ○

God Loves You: The Resurrection Is the Proof!

Jesus did not die for Himself; He died for you and me. It was the greatest act of love in all of history: Jesus died for people who didn't even know Him or care!

We all need forgiveness, and we need someone who is innocent to pay for our sins. Jesus, the pure and holy Son of God, took the blame for our sins and paid the price so that we could be forgiven and enjoy a brand-new start! Have you messed up? Have things gone wrong? This is your time—right now—to receive forgiveness for your sin and healing for your brokenness. Before you were born, God knew what you would need. Because Jesus loved you, you can start a new life and leave your past behind. He will help you overcome every obstacle that you will face! Let God wipe your slate clean.

This is the beginning of your new day! Decide now. Receive Jesus. Know that He is waiting to embrace you and celebrate your life!

Are you thinking, *Well, how does He feel about me with all of the bad things that I've done?* He loves you and when you admit your wrongs and turn away from them, He will forgive you of them forever! Actually, He loved and forgave you before you were born! He only requires that you repent. Simply pray, *Jesus, forgive me. I receive Your love.* Let it happen in your life—now! Here's an incredible story of what Jesus can do!

"I'm Saved! Love Healed and Delivered Me!"

The Kirby McCauley Story

Kirby remembers the adult whispers about her father's "strange relationship" with her, but as a little girl she had no clue they were talking about sexual abuse. He died when she was ten years old, and she still can't pinpoint when the abuse started.

"Quite a few cousins and younger siblings lived at home with us, and they were being molested too.

"Since my mom had been molested during her childhood too, I think it was hard for her to acknowledge the problem and stop it."

Kirby grew up in a family of nine in a home with no love. "I didn't know what love was," Kirby said. After her dad died, Kirby's mother had to leave the children in the care of the eldest sister while she went to work each day. She was only twelve herself, so she really couldn't provide parental guidance to her siblings.

"We started to experiment sexually during that time, and we did a lot of things that the average child probably wouldn't do," Kirby said.

"I began to 'experiment' with a guy who was seventeen years old. I'm sure he knew what he was doing, but I didn't.

"Mom always worked, and when she finally got home at night, she didn't have much time or energy for us. When Mom finally realized what had happened and told me (I was going to have a baby), I was already five months pregnant but still playing out in the backyard with my brothers and sisters!"

Despite having a baby, Kirby still didn't know how she had gotten pregnant. Predictably, she had a second baby at sixteen. Her experimentation also led to drug addiction and truancy. Eventually, it even led Kirby into prostitution.

When Kirby's mother learned her daughter was pregnant the second time, she said, "Kirby, if you go out there and you have those kids, then you're gonna have to provide for them." So Kirby moved out of her mother's house and into a relationship at age seventeen.

"This guy noticed I wanted a father figure in my young son's life.

He started coming over and acted as if he would meet that need, but he actually wanted an 'exchange.'

"He would invest his money if I would provide sex. I thought it was love, because love to me was sex. I had never known anything else.

"He was a drug dealer and his activities put us all in jeopardy. Several times people came to my home with handguns or shotguns looking for him. I lived in constant fear for almost three years."

The man beat Kirby, and on the last day before she escaped from that relationship, he threatened her children as well. She slipped out of the back door and called the police from her neighbor's house. They took her boyfriend to jail, and they also took her children into protective custody.

> ## I couldn't help it. In my joy, I just kept saying, "I'm saved! I'm saved!"

"I'll never forget that night. I was already an alcoholic, so I left my apartment to find something to drink. I wanted to drown my pain with alcohol.

"It was hard seeing my kids placed in such a bad situation. I felt as if I couldn't do anything about it. Then I was introduced to cocaine, and my behavior and personality quickly took a more dangerous turn. I wasn't even myself. I could tell the addiction was taking over, but I didn't know what to do."

Some friends invited Kirby to church services sometimes, but she always came back unchanged…because she still hadn't encountered Jesus personally.

"After I lost the kids, I smoked crack and drank beer for four straight months. Then I found out I was four months pregnant!

"It didn't change a thing; I still tried to stay high on crack cocaine for the entire nine months of my pregnancy to erase my pain.

"Things got so bad that when I went to the crack house to buy drugs, I moved in there! It was awful."

Kirby didn't want to face her past or her miserable present because it brought her torment. She wanted to drown out those thoughts by any means possible, but time was running out. She discovered that even when she injected crack cocaine she wasn't getting high anymore. Kirby began to walk the streets at night, crying out to "somebody, anybody" for help.

"I'll never forget the nineteenth of June," Kirby said. "I was walking down a street when I heard some live music that just seemed to draw me, and I didn't know why." A woman noticed that Kirby was crying and asked what was going on.

"I thought I wanted to kill myself, but something inside me really wanted to live. This lady said, 'Well, just come down here. We have a street ministry.'

"I don't remember what the message was, but afterward a guy called me up and started praying over me. That's when a feeling came over me. Something literally came up out of my body! All of the heaviness that had been weighing on me just disappeared!

"I just kept saying, 'I'm saved!' It must have been God, because I didn't even know what 'I'm saved' meant. I couldn't help it. In my joy, I just kept saying, 'I'm saved! I'm saved!'

"Today I can tell you that through His resurrection Jesus saved me from hell, from the dark world, and from the destructive hurts and pain I was experiencing. He literally saved me from 'where I was going.'

"God's love for me is the greatest thing that could have ever happened. Love is what healed and delivered me!" (Adapted from videotaped interview.)

○ ○ ○ ○ ○

Embrace Jesus, Embrace Your New Life

There are no limits to God's power! It is the power made available through the resurrection of Jesus. And that same resurrection power can be right where you are this very moment!

Do you sense the Holy Spirit drawing near to you right now? He may be whispering to your heart, "You can have a resurrection in your life too! I can raise the dreams that have died. I can restore what has been destroyed, wasted, or ruined."

Jesus can resurrect broken families, rebuild destroyed marriages, and restore wasted lives. Just pray, "Yes, Lord. I receive what You did for me." Simply believe and receive. Put your trust in Jesus and receive eternal life from Him through the power of the Resurrection.

Are you wondering, *How do I believe?*

You begin by believing what you have heard from the Word of God: Jesus was declared to be the Son of God by His resurrection from the dead (see Romans 1:4). Only in Jesus can you know that you will live with God forever!

"How do you know?" you ask. Jesus puts His Spirit on the inside of you. He is God's living "witness" or confirmation in your heart. It produces an unshakable "knowing" that you belong to God as one of His children, a member of God's family.

God is saying to you, *I desire you and love you so much that I gave My only Son so that you who believe in Him would not perish—would not go to hell—would not be destroyed, but would have everlasting life!* (see John 3:16).

Once your life is under new management from heaven, God's resurrection life inside you transforms who you are and gives you hope, peace, joy, and confidence.

Why wait to accept this gift of eternal life from God? Just pray this prayer out loud: "Jesus, I believe You are the Son of God. I believe You died for me. I believe You were raised from the dead, and I confess You as my Lord. This day, Jesus, I receive Your resurrection power inside of me."

Now find another Christian, and tell him or her what God has done in your life! Find a church that preaches the Bible, and study the Bible for yourself (begin with the gospel of John in the New Testament).

Finally, make sure you talk to the Lord every day. He is the Friend who will never leave you. He always hears and has your very best in mind.

Receive your good news! This is the new beginning you have longed for!

Welcome to the family!

2

Overcoming Fear and Anxiety

What is your biggest **fear**?

fear of darkness (lygophobia)

fear of spiders (arachnophobia)

fear of sharp objects, like needles (aichmophobia)

Scared yet?

fear of ninjas ("ninjaphobia")

fear of clowns (coulrophobia)

fear of your **mother-in-law** (pentheraphobia)

How about now?

fear of being **alone** (isolophobia)

fear of poverty (peniaphobia)

fear of disease (pathophobia)

Yikes!

What is bigger than your biggest fear?

God!

God hasn't given you a spirit of fear but of power, love, and a peaceful mind, so take a *deep breath*. Relax. **Fear not.** God is bigger than your biggest fear!

Almost every week a headline on one of those grocery store tabloids shouts: "Shocking Prophecies of the Future!" But does anyone ever check up on the validity of these predictions?

A prophet once predicted that people in the future would worry about what they were going to eat, what they were going to drink, and what they were going to wear! He said they would be constantly consumed with worry about their basic needs and safety in troubled times.

This prophet's predictions date back about two thousand years, and *this* prophet's predictions were right. The prophet was Jesus, and He also said that anyone who trusted Him should not have to worry about these things.

No matter what you see on TV or the Internet, you can overcome any anxiety, fear, or panic that tries to come your way! I can understand why you maybe struggle with torment and anxiety with all the trouble in the world, but I have good news!

This is your day to walk free of it! (And if you are already enjoying freedom through Jesus, then this is your day to help others get through their hard times.) Jesus encouraged us to trust Him and reminded us that we can't make ourselves even one inch taller by thinking or worrying about it. He taught us that our heavenly Father knows what we need and He will provide for every one of those needs (see Matthew 6:25–33). Jesus pointed out that birds don't sow seed, plow fields, or gather crops into barns like farmers do. They don't do any of those things, but they don't go hungry. Why? Their heavenly Father feeds them.

> **A**bove all, you need to understand how much God cares about you!

Have you noticed all of the berries that remain on bushes and shrubs, even during the winter? When God made this planet, He even made provision for the birds and countless foraging animals. Jesus said: "Look at the lilies and how they grow. They don't work or make their clothing, yet Solomon in all his glory was not dressed as beautifully as they are. And if God cares so wonderfully for flowers that are here today and gone tomorrow, *won't he more surely care for you?*" (Matthew 6:28–30, NLT, emphasis added).

If God can dress flowers like that, then surely He can make sure you have something to eat!

Above all, you need to understand how much God cares about you! He loves you, He has a plan for your life, and He will provide for your needs. Thousands of years ago He called Himself Jehovah-Jireh, which is the Hebrew word used to characterize the Lord as the One who sees ahead and provides for us accordingly.

If you grew up under good circumstances, then as a child you trusted your father and mother. You knew they were thinking of you and would provide for you to the best of their ability. If you didn't have a mom and dad like that, then you are about to meet the heavenly Father who never fails or betrays and who always keeps His word!

The heavenly Father owns this planet and all of the universe (and beyond). You are His child and He has been thinking of and preparing for you. When you know Him, you have confidence in Him.

Remember that Jesus said if God cares for the birds and clothes the lilies across the world, then how much more will He take care of you? Allow that truth to sink deep inside of you. *God will take care of you!* Believe it. Expect it! Then God will provide you with direction on what to do next.

Before we started our own ministry, for many years my wife, Sharon, and I attended church with a wonderful friend. I didn't realize he was married because I had never met his wife.

My friend was about fifty years old when I learned that he was married. He explained that she suffered from agoraphobia—a fear of open places or unfamiliar surroundings or situations. She was so afraid of these things that she kept herself locked in their house, where she spent most of her time in bed with all the curtains closed and the bedcovers pulled over her head.

Things hadn't always been that way. God had blessed this couple with children, and life was good early in their married life. However, when bad things happened and troubles came, she didn't know how to deal with them and became a recluse.

When Sharon and I started a new church on Easter Sunday in 1981, I preached on the Year of Jubilee. This happened to be the fiftieth birthday of my friend's wife, so she decided to risk everything and come to church that morning. In my sermon I explained that *jubilee* speaks of a new beginning of God's grace and mercy, when He restores what the devil has stolen. This woman made a decision that day: "I'm coming out of my fear. I'm going to trust God for freedom!"

The change was amazing! This lady and her husband began visiting the sick in hospitals and continued this ministry for our church for twenty-five years!

How can someone whose crippling fear prevented her from leaving her house suddenly decide to go out into the wider world to visit and pray for sick and hurting people in hospitals? What changed her life? How did she go from a life of isolated darkness to a life spent reaching out to others in the love of God—operating in the environments that used to terrify her?

She believed God could help her, and then she discovered His plan for her life!

What about you? Do you ever say, "I could do some great stuff too, but you don't understand how afraid I am"?

Do you remember how God takes care of the birds and the flowers? How He has promised to take even better care of you? God has plans for you! No matter what fears, troubles, or problems you face right now, trust Him. He can help you overcome those anxieties! This is God's message to you: *fear not!*

Alone and Afraid...Until God's Word Became My Best Friend!

CHERYL'S STORY

Nine years ago I started having panic attacks, but I didn't realize it! I would go to work and be fine during the day, because there were lots of people around and I was always busy. Then I'd come home in the evening, rush through my dinner, and leave. I just couldn't stand being home by myself.

I'd window shop, go to different stores, and only return home after ten or eleven o'clock at night. I would just sleep for a few hours, because I knew that sometime in the middle of the night I'd wake up in a cold sweat, frightened out of my mind.

Fear overwhelmed me, and I felt like I was all alone. One passage in the Amplified Bible became my most powerful weapon against fear: "For God did not give us a spirit of timidity (of cowardice, of craven and cringing and fawning fear), but [He has given us a spirit] of power and of love and of calm and well-balanced mind and discipline and self-control" (2 Timothy 1:7).

When fear began to overwhelm me, I knew I had to get into God's Word, and it became my best friend. Whenever I read this powerful passage from 2 Timothy, I'm free!

○ ○ ○ ○ ○

ONE KEY RELEASES EVERYTHING!

When Jesus taught about living the worry-free life, He said (in my own words), "Your heavenly Father knows everything that you need, so why should you worry?" He went on to say, "He will give you all you need from day to day if you live for him and make the Kingdom of God your primary concern" (Matthew 6:33, NLT).

That is the key that releases everything God intends for you! Jesus is the King, and you want the King to rule your life. This means surrendering your life to Jesus and saying, "Be the Lord and Ruler of my life. Take charge." When you do that, you are in His total care.

When recruits join a branch of the armed forces, they must make a total commitment to their country and to a term of service. At that point the military provides all their essential clothing, shelter, training, and transportation. And so it is when you commit all to the King and the kingdom of God: He provides for everything in your life—the spiritual, the mental, the physical. You can count on it: God will keep His promise and take care of you! The Amplified Bible describes this powerful promise written by the apostle Peter:

> [Cast] the whole of your care [all your anxieties, all your worries, all your concerns, once and for all] on Him, for He cares for you affectionately and cares about you watchfully. (1 Peter 5:7, AMP)

No one will ever care for you like Jesus! Sharon and I have learned from years of experience that God makes a way. Whether we faced a need in housing, clothing, transportation, or ministry, God was there for us. And He will make a way in your life too!

Cast every care, worry, and fear upon the Lord. Say, "Lord, I trust You. I'm going to seek You first, and I believe that You will add to me everything that I need."

Break Free and Stay Free by Speaking the Word

THE STORY OF JEFF GOFORTH

I suffered in silence for years. Dread, fear, and torment consumed me, but the isolation was the worst.

My journey of fear began when I was a young boy struggling with anxiety and worry. I found a spot on my side one time, and I thought, *Oh, my gosh. I'm gonna die!* I contemplated death for days afterward. After a while, I kind of blew it off, and I thought, *Well, it's probably somewhat normal.*

Unfortunately, I stopped thinking I was normal as time progressed in my life. I began to realize that I was really struggling with anxiety.

Six years ago [2003], I began to have debilitating panic attacks that could hit me almost anytime and in any situation. Whether I was sitting in church or working at my desk at the office, the thought could come, *You're gonna die right here!* Panic would overwhelm me; my palms would sweat, and my heart would race.

No area of life was immune from attack. I was afraid of getting a disease, I was afraid someone would break into the house and kill me, and I was afraid of driving my car. Often while I was driving, panic would hit. I had to literally pull over.

Sometimes I would be walking in a public place when suddenly a thought would trigger paralyzing fear. I'd think, *You're gonna pass out right here! Everybody's going to find out who you really are, and you'll look like a fool.*

I was too embarrassed to tell anyone what I was going through. I was sure they wouldn't or couldn't understand. When I finally shared a little of my ordeal with people, they would say something like, "Oh, just deal with it. You'll be fine." But I wasn't fine.

When a panic attack struck during a church service, I actually thought I was dying. I told my wife, "Honey, I have got to get out of here!"

An incident with my son forced me to face the seriousness of my panic problem. It's extremely difficult to talk about this even to this day. I tried to take my son with me to a video store (he was about three or four years old at the time). When I walked up to the counter and tried to check out, I had a panic attack.

I had to run to the bathroom—and take my little boy with me. It really bothered me. I thought, *What is wrong with me? I can't even be a father to my son because this stuff has gotten so bad.* There I was in total humiliation, locked in the bathroom with my son. I was thinking, *There has to be a way out! There has to be. This cannot be my life!* I just wanted it to stop.

> **P**anic would overwhelm me; my palms
> would sweat, and my heart would race.

After years of silent suffering, I reached the point where I told my wife, "Honey, this is what has been going on. I'm having anxiety attacks and I'm really struggling. I need help. You've got to do one of two things: either take me to the hospital or have someone come pray for me."

She called someone from the church, and they came to pray for me. After years of hiding my struggles and pain, I finally opened up and described what I had been going through. That night when they prayed for me, it was as if something broke inside of me!

A lot of people say to me, "You had panic attacks and now you're better. How did you do it? How did you get set free?" I answer, "Prayer broke it, and the Word of God keeps it there."

I wrote key passages from God's Word on three-by-five-inch index cards, read them over and over again, and I began speaking them out: "For God has not given me a spirit of fear, but He's given a spirit of power and of love and of a calm and a well-balanced mind" [based on 2 Timothy 1:7]; "Casting your cares upon the Lord" [based on 1 Peter 5:7]; and "Be anxious for nothing" [Philippians 4:6].

Perhaps you've heard these verses before, but "faith comes by hearing" [Romans 10:17]. Peace came when I heard those Scriptures spoken by my own mouth. It didn't happen instantly. Peace came as I stayed in the Word and faithfully meditated on God's truth. I still speak the Word. That is what got me free, and that is what keeps me free.

○ ○ ○ ○ ○

FIND FAITH IN CHRIST...AND LOSE YOUR WORRY!

Whatever you're going through, God can help you get through it! It's time to overcome anxieties and fears about finances, physical problems, family situations, and relationships. Jesus cares about you, so cast your cares upon Him. He already knows what you need. Just put His kingdom and His right way of doing things first.

In his letter to the Philippians, the apostle Paul said not to worry about anything but pray about everything. He urged us to give thanks when we pray and have faith that the peace of God will guard our hearts and our minds through Christ Jesus (see Philippians 4:4–7).

Don't "pray and worry." Pray and give thanks, and allow God's peace to fill your mind and your heart.

It doesn't matter how violent or hopeless the storm of your life may be, as long as Jesus is in the boat with you! He is the Prince of Peace, and peace goes where He goes—in your storm, in the economy, in your neighborhood! Trust Him. God will make a way for you! He is faithful to keep His promises and to do what He has spoken.

Early in our ministry in Tulsa, we assumed a bank loan on a huge building measuring sixty-five thousand square feet. It was a difficult time for us. The building had housed a huge car dealership handling seven different brands—until it went bankrupt. God spoke to me that this was where we were to begin, so we assumed the $3.3 million property note.

A lot of people attended the church, but we were facing an interest rate of nearly 15 percent. So we decided to sell the building and get into a better position financially. Two and a half years went by without a single offer. No one even visited or called! Things looked bleak. We'd ruined the property as a potential car dealership by changing it into a church and school. And since it didn't look like a church, other churches didn't want the building either.

I faced some of the worst worry and anxiety I've ever experienced, until the Lord began to speak to me about the lion, the bear, and the giant in David's life. David said that he had killed a lion and killed a bear and "I can overcome the giant" (see 1 Samuel 17:37).

God told me that He would make a way for our church to overcome this building problem if we would begin to sow and plant our seed (our money and resources) to help others and to reach out to the hurting. Our lion, or first victory, would be to find an interim site on a rental basis so that we could move our ministry to a new home. Our bear, the second major victory, would be to sell the large building and property. Our giant would be to move forward on a cash basis from that point on.

> You can defeat the greatest fear of all—the fear of death!

My worry ended and the miracles started to happen! We found an empty school building that met our needs, and after seven attempts with the school system, we finally were able to rent the building, and we overcame our lion.

Shortly after that we had some interest in the former dealership site (after thirty months of noninterest). It just happened to be an inquiry from officials at Walmart's corporate headquarters. They wanted that site for the city's first Sam's Club location! I understand it became one of the most productive Sam's Club stores in the nation during the first few years after it opened. We used the proceeds from the sale to pay off everything the church owed, and we even had about $200,000 left over!

Then it was time to face the giant. Our giant was to buy land and build debt free, without borrowing money from the bank. As you recall, David took five small stones from a creek bed and hurled one at the giant Goliath. God said to us, *Plant your seeds of faith and love into other people, other ministries, and into missions. Then I'll bring down the giant.* He did. From 1985 to the present, our ministry has operated and grown on a debt-free basis. That is how we have purchased new land, built new buildings, and launched new ministries locally and worldwide.

Be encouraged! It may take you a few years, but you can come out of debt and break free of financial bondage and the fear it brings. I know what it feels like to wake up in the middle of the night with overwhelming pressure, wondering, *What are we going to do?* But I also know that when we trusted God and did what He said, God brought us out on top. He will do the same for you.

You also can defeat the greatest fear of all—the fear of death! We touched on this in the previous chapter, and we'll look at it again because many of the fears we battle in life stem from our fear of death. That fear must leave when you receive Jesus Christ as your Lord and Savior! If you've never received Him into your life, then why not do it now?

Simply say this prayer out loud: "Jesus, I believe You died for me. I believe You were raised from the dead. I confess You as my Lord and Savior. Take over my life."

If you prayed this prayer, then today marks a new beginning in your life! Your time to triumph over fear and anxiety has come! Enjoy your new freedom. And never forget how much God cares for you!

3

You Can Make a Difference

Yes, **you**...
> you with the lousy singing voice
> you with the shady past
> you with the lack of fashion sense
> you!

You are God's workmanship—created, purposed, **destined** for good works.
> You = God's feet.
> You = God's hands.
> You = God's voice...
>> ...on the other end of the line.

So **look** around.
> Someone needs your help.
> Someone needs *you*.

You can make **all the difference** in the world!

Who, me?"

"What can I do? I'm not anything special. Nobody needs what I have to offer."

"Why me? I just can't do that."

You are not the first to doubt or question God's judgment in choosing you, and you won't be the last.

You share your question with some world-class hesitators like Noah, Abraham, Moses, Samuel, Esther, David, Solomon, Isaiah, Elijah and Elisha, Ruth and Naomi, Mary the mother of Jesus, and the twelve disciples.

It isn't the initial self-doubt that will defeat you; it is the failure to deal with it that leads to your surrender to disobedience. God knows you can make a difference in someone else's life! Wherever you live, there is someone nearby who needs your help. You were born for a holy purpose, and God created you to flourish in this exact moment of human history, right in the exact place that you call home today.

You are part of God's answer for how to heal our broken world. He specifically designed you to meet needs on this planet and to touch the lives of real people who may not even know who are. He gave you certain gifts, talents, and abilities, and He has even helped you pass through experiences that will help you help others! Good times. Bad times. God uses them all to help you relate to people facing similar situations and carrying similar hopes in life.

Our culture and our human nature encourage us to live for Number One—to look out for our own interests. Every decision and activity of ours seems to revolve around one question: *What's in it for me?* Then we wonder why our life is so unfulfilled!

God sends you in exactly the opposite direction to find fulfillment. When His love floods your life, you naturally begin to ask, *What can I give of my life to help someone else?*

Fulfillment comes when you discover the divine purpose for which you were born! Once you discover the passion God planted inside of you and you connect your purpose and passion with the opportunity to touch another person's life, supernatural joy is unleashed!

Do you want to experience genuine fulfillment? It can happen right now! Simply pray, *Lord, guide my steps. Show me where to give my life away.*

> **W**herever you live, there is someone nearby who needs your help.

Those steps may take you into your neighborhood or lead you back to the office. He may send you into a nearby area where people are suffering or hurting, or He may send you to the most needy parts of your city or region, which may include a hospital, a nursing home, or the homeless and indigent scraping out an existence under a bridge.

Everyone and anyone can make a difference! God did not create a single insignificant person. Maybe you have never really believed that because you think of yourself as unimportant or not particularly valuable. The truth is, because of who your Creator is, you are awesome! Like David, you should say, "I will praise You, for I am fearfully and wonderfully made!" (Psalm 139:14).

Dare to open your heart and declare, "Lord, take over my life and use me for Your purpose." From that moment forward, you will become powerful and anointed by God to make a difference! This is the time you've been waiting for: awaken to the dream God put inside of you!

Perhaps you are still thinking, *How can I make a difference? Who actually needs me?* Jesus answered those questions the day He was asked, "Who is my neighbor?" He told the story of a man who was mugged by thieves while walking between the cities of Jerusalem and Jericho. They beat him until he was unconscious and then left him bleeding and dying beside a heavily traveled road.

A priest came by and saw the wounded man in the ditch, but instead of running to his aid, he moved over to the other side of the road. Then a slightly lower-ranking member of the priestly class who served in the temple also walked by. He also chose not to get involved and crossed to the other side of the road.

Finally a Samaritan approached the man in the ditch. This man was from the politically incorrect class of people who had mixed ethnic and religious backgrounds—he was someone the religiously privileged people would avoid in all situations. When this Samaritan man saw the Jewish man abandoned in the ditch, he turned aside, dismounted from his donkey, and began to treat the man's wounds. Then he put him on the donkey and took him to an inn. Once he had made the man comfortable, he went to the innkeeper and prepaid the man's bill for room and board—plus any special care required until the man was fully recovered.

Then Jesus asked the person who had posed the original question,

"Which one of these men was the wounded man's neighbor?" (see Luke 10:36). Even though the man didn't want to admit that an unworthy Samaritan could be the story's hero, he grudgingly allowed that the good neighbor was the Samaritan.

The story of the good Samaritan, whose compassion allowed him to make a difference, has been retold around the world countless times over the last two thousand years! What a difference he made. He touched not only the man who was robbed but also the millions of people who have heard that story in every century since.

When you or I touch even one life, the ripple effect of that compassionate act can impact thousands of lives. Consider the story of a small-statured Albanian girl named Agnes who felt a strong call to missionary service at the age of twelve and actually began her work at age eighteen. In 1948 she received permission to devote all of her energy to sharing love, kindness, food, help, and shelter to the very poorest people in India. By the time she died in 1997 at age eighty-seven, she had impacted the whole world with her determination to affect one life at a time.

Perhaps you know her by another name: Mother Teresa.

This tiny lady with a big heart started with only a handful of people, but when she died, her personal campaign had become a mighty movement with 610 missions in 123 countries and over 100,000 volunteer helpers from around the world!

> **Y**ou are a perfect match for the
> purposes of God!

You can make a difference too. Have you asked this question—it is one of the most important questions in your life: "God, what do You want me to do? Where do I start?"

Don't wait. I encourage you to get started now! Touch someone's life today—whether you do it through a phone call, a text message, an e-mail, a personal visit, or just by giving somebody some encouragement, help, or strength in some way. Sometimes it only takes a few words, such as "I love you" or "I care about you." Or how about, "Please forgive me"?

Remember, as a Christian with God at the center of your life, you have more to offer than human encouragement and assistance—as good as they are. Because you have the power of the Holy Spirit residing in you, it may only take a single word to totally change a person's life!

So, what gives you significance? Think about what Jesus said: "He who finds his life will lose it, and he who loses his life for My sake will find it" (Matthew 10:39). Jesus conveys this truth in three other places in the gospels—Matthew 16:25, Mark 8:35, and Luke 9:24.

Jesus was talking about significance! He was warning us that there are consequences when we selfishly choose to go our own way and do our own thing. On the other hand, when we choose what God has for us—even though we may want to go another direction—then we will find the life we were born to live! This is the most important fact about significance we will ever need to understand!

God has a plan and purpose for you—to do the good works He has prepared for you. The apostle Paul said, "For we are His workmanship, created in Christ Jesus for good works, which God prepared beforehand so that we would walk in them" (Ephesians 2:10, NASB). In other words, God created you for those good works, and He prepared the good works for you.

So you are a perfect match for these purposes of God! How's that for being significant? The good works were prepared by God ahead of time, so they aren't going anywhere. That means that you are the one in motion right now. Either you are moving toward the things God has prepared for you, or you are moving away from them.

Don't hold back or move away. Do everything in your power to follow God's lead. Once you discover those good works God has prepared for you, then you will experience the fulfillment you've always longed for! "This is what I was born to do. So this is why I was put on the planet!" you will say. It's one of the most exciting things you will ever experience.

A TOUGH QUESTION

As a young college student, I was sitting on a bunk bed in an athletic dorm when this thought came to me: *What have you ever done for anyone else?*

Only a few months earlier I had received Jesus Christ as my Lord and Savior, so I had just become spiritually alive. The question echoed throughout my entire being: *What have I ever done for anyone else?*

What can I do? I thought. Then the Lord said to me, "Why don't you reach out to little children playing basketball at the Boys Club?"

I had fond memories of growing up and going to the Boys Club, so I applied to be a basketball coach. The experience of working with those nine- and ten-year-old children that year began to transform my life. I realized I really did have something to give!

You really have something to give too. I don't know what or where it might be—perhaps you will give others your time, talents, or resources. All I know is that it will involve giving, and it may be in ways or places no one else would think of.

Perhaps you've been uniquely equipped to reach out to the homeless or to children who have been abandoned. You may have a singing voice that is used supernaturally to inspire others or a heart of compassion to comfort those who are hurting and suffering.

Whatever and wherever it is, we have God's Word on it: there is a place for you. You can make a difference. You were not born to waste your life—you have a purpose.

A ninety-one-year-old woman once shared, "God spoke to me, telling me to go into a nursing home and give people hugs." Think about that: God has given this precious woman, at ninety-one, a *new* ministry of touching people who may have been forgotten! She is God's representative sent to love people who otherwise might not have a single visitor for weeks on end. This woman doesn't let her age or circumstances get in the way: she is too busy making a difference in the lives of others.

You see, God wants to show you how you can make a difference too! It happened to Ben Key one day as he drove to work as usual—only to encounter the unusual. It was the day God inserted him directly into the life of someone in desperate need.

The Guy Wanted to Jump...so I Climbed Out over the Guardrail

THE STORY OF BEN KEY

We were on the 71st Street Bridge crossing the Arkansas River when I realized something was not right. I was on my way to drop off my six- and seven-year-olds at school, and I told them to start praying with me.

Then I looked across the traffic lanes to the opposite side of the bridge, and I saw a guy standing outside of the guardrail. In fact, he was outside the chain-link barrier, just looking down. Suddenly I felt like I needed to get over there quickly.

But we were in traffic, moving away on the opposite side of the bridge. I'd have to make a U-turn to go back to where this guy was.

I called 911, but there was no question in my mind—I knew I would have to go help him. And I knew that from the way he looked that something wasn't right.

After I dialed 911, the operator told me that quite a few other people had called about the guy. I'm not sure why no one else had stopped.

My first thought when I saw him was, *This guy wants to jump!* That made it even stranger to me that no one else had stopped, especially the people who were on his side of the bridge.

When I finally drove up to the guy's location, I stopped the car and put on my hazard lights. After I checked the kids, I got out of the car and climbed over the guardrail.

I went up to the fence where this man was located and was shocked by what I saw. He was perched on a narrow ledge outside of the barrier fence with both arms wrapped around the top of the fence. The ledge could only support his heels, and he just kept looking down toward the river.

There was just a very little ledge for him to stand on. He didn't even look at me when I walked up behind him. He was focused on the river below him, and he looked very somber.

When I followed his gaze and looked down, there was nothing below him but rocks—a full forty-five feet below! So I just started trying to make conversation—to be friendly.

My first thought was to take him to our church and try to find somebody there, like our pastor, who could pray with this guy and counsel him. But I knew I couldn't start there. So I just began talking to this guy; I asked if he would like to go talk and get a cup of coffee or something. Finally he agreed.

I knew I would have to help him climb back over the fence, but there was not much room for him to stand, let alone move or climb anywhere. Afraid he might fall, I just put my arms around his from my side of the fence and helped him over. After he got in the car with us, he seemed calm and friendly. But I could tell he had a lot on his mind.

After we turned around and headed toward the church, we saw an ambulance plus police cruisers coming from every direction toward the bridge.

"I think the police and the ambulance are for you," I told my guest. Then I flagged down one of the police officers.

They questioned the man and took him in the ambulance to a hospital for examination. That evening I talked to the police officer I'd met on the bridge, and he said the man was a Christian. He had experienced some rough things recently and had planned to commit suicide.

I'd just been talking to the kids in our nightly devotions about the good Samaritan who helped somebody in need. This miracle really stood out to them. Now they know they can make a difference by reaching out to help others.

God gives each of us opportunities to help others who genuinely need help. It was awesome that God put us in the right place at the right time to actually make a difference in that man's life.

○ ○ ○ ○ ○

YOU HAVE A GOD-GIVEN PURPOSE!

You can make a difference! Is this your day to find your place on the earth? If you haven't done so already, it's time to begin fulfilling your purpose and live out the dream that God has for you. Are you willing to release the passion, energy, and the drive that God has for your life? Begin to do things that change and touch someone else's life!

I believe everyone is born with a holy purpose, but we often undermine that purpose by comparing ourselves to other people. Have you ever said to yourself something like, *I don't have the personality like her,* or, *I can't speak like he does.*

It doesn't matter. God made each of us special. You were designed like no one else. No two fingerprints are alike. No two voiceprints will ever match, and no two sunsets, snowflakes, or grains of sand have ever been alike! God is a God of infinite variety, and you are unique.

- Stop comparing yourself with others.
- Stop discounting what God counts precious—your life.
- Remember that somebody needs your love right where you are—someone whom God has appointed for you to touch!
  That is your assignment.

I know a man who was once defined by his horrific background and terrible experiences in life. But after he came out of jail, he heard about God's love and grace; he learned that God could still use him. He surrendered his life to Jesus Christ and allowed the Lord to help him deal with the shame, guilt, and condemnation that he felt.

Today, Phil Brown picks up homeless and indigent people living under the bridges and on our streets in Tulsa. He provides them with warm food, shelter, and the love of God through our Dream Center. Phil understands God's compassion—God gave Phil a wonderful wife, restored the years that had been devastated, and now is using him for the glory of God. He can do the same for you!

Think of everything God has working in your life: His love, mercy, grace, forgiveness, goodness, truth, and promises! Now open up your eyes, look around, and ask yourself: *Who could I love? Who could I care about?*

My father died in 1974, and I joined my brothers, Jack and Charles, to help Mom and attend his memorial service in south Arkansas. Just before I was to return to my home, I told my mom, "You can spend the rest of your life in a rocking chair, or you can get up and do something for someone else."

She may have thought those were tough words, but they were just what she needed to hear. At the time Mom was working in a radio station as a secretary each day from 8:00 a.m. to 5:00 p.m., but the Monday following the memorial service, she put in eight hours at the station and then went directly to a nursing home and began to reach out and pray for people! She went from room to room and introduced herself to residents she didn't know, and one by one, she talked to them and loved on them.

Later on she told me, "You know, I've never really experienced grief like I hear other people talk about." What happened? When she gave her love away, love came back to her.

Years ago I heard a story (as told by Joel Barker) about a young boy who noticed that starfish had washed up on a seashore. He began to pick up the starfish and throw them back into the water.

An older gentleman came up to him and said, "What are you doing?"

The young boy said, "Well, I'm saving starfish."

The man looked down the beach and said, "There are hundreds, even thousands of them. You're not going to make a difference, son. You could never save them all."

You could see the disappointment in the little boy's face. Finally, he stooped down and picked up one more starfish. He looked at it and then said, "It will make a difference to this one." And he tossed it back into the ocean.

You and I were washed up on the shores of humanity until Jesus came from heaven and picked us up. We can live again because He put us back in the ocean of God's love. This is the grace and the mercy of God extended especially to us.

This is your time to say, *Yes, Lord, allow Your love to flow through me. Help me make a difference in someone else's life today. Be the Lord of my life. In Your name I pray. Amen.*

Now get ready for some real excitement! God *will* use you to make a difference!

4

The Power
of Your Words

Do you think before you **speak**?
> Or do you speak before you think?
> Consider this: The tongue is like the rudder of a boat.
>> Where it goes, the boat follows.

Now imagine **your life** is a great big boat.
What kind of words steer your ship?
> words that heal
> words that build
> words that create
> words that encourage
> words that protect
> words that mend
> words that forgive
> words that uplift
> words that unite

words that humor
words that restore
words that rescue

Or…
words that destroy
words that ruin
words that wound
words that humiliate
words that offend
words that scar
words that hurt
words that divorce
words that abuse
words that terrorize

What you **say** = where you go.

Change your words = **change** your course.

Your future changes when you really pay attention to the warning in the book of Proverbs about being "trapped by what you said, ensnared by the words of your mouth" (6:2, NIV). That actually goes both ways. When you choose words from the Word of God and speak His truth about your life and future, then you will be snared by good things. But when you speak fear, death, calamity, tragedy, doubt, disaster, or hate—all those things begin to become a part of your life.

You can change your course by speaking the Word properly. Perhaps you are thinking, *But I don't understand this!*

Do you understand the detailed mathematical underpinnings of the law of gravity? Yet you clearly understand how gravity can work for you or against you! For instance, is it easier to slide down a slide at the park or to climb back up to the top? Is it easier to carry a cup of water in an upright glass or an upside-down glass?

In the same way, the law of what you say is a biblical truth and a principle in the universe: the things you say from your heart will prepare the way in your life. They produce things related to either death or life.

In fact, the Bible says that the tongue is like the bit in a horse's mouth (see James 3:2–3). A bit is made of one or more pieces of smooth metal that you can hold in the palm of your hand. It fits inside the horse's mouth toward the back where there are no teeth. The bit is attached to a bridle—a headpiece made of leather or woven material that slips over a horse's head—and lines, or reins, go from the ends of the bit to the rider's hands. Although a horse may weigh hundreds of pounds more than you do, that tiny bit allows you to direct the horse wherever you want it to go.

James goes on to say that the tongue is also like the rudder of a ship (see James 3:4–5). A rudder is a steering mechanism that is often totally invisible because most or all of it is under the surface of the water. It is very small in comparison to the ship it steers. Yet even though that rudder is very small, it can guide the massive ship whichever way the helmsman or captain directs it to go.

In comparison to the size of your body, your tongue may be very small. Yet like the bit in a horse's mouth or a rudder on a ship, the words it produces direct the path of your life. This principle is described in both the Old and New Testaments of the Bible. According to your words, you can go up or you can go down. You can walk into abundant life, or you can go into death.

> There is power in the declaration of your words.

You speak life into your future every time you declare the Word of life and the Word of faith over your life. Things happen when you declare over yourself and your family powerful words of joy and victory taken directly from God's divine Word.

Think about what would happen to your average day if you began each morning with the declaration: "I have a reason to live! God has a purpose for my life, and I am going to finish my course. I am going to do what God has assigned me to do!"

This isn't something you should put off until tomorrow.

If you learn to speak the Word of God from your heart in faith using your tongue, you will guide your life into a pathway of blessing. The combination of believing and speaking is key to the vital process of salvation. The Bible says, "For with the heart one believes unto righteousness, and with the mouth confession is made unto salvation" (Romans 10:10). You can't even get saved without believing and speaking! Consider this: "For 'whoever calls on the name of the LORD shall be saved' " (Romans 10:13, where Paul quotes Joel 2:32).

Clearly there is power in the declaration of your words. The words of faith that you speak can set you free or help you escape disaster. I experienced this personally several years ago when I learned to fly a plane. On one occasion, I took a long-distance trip by myself and became trapped in a violent storm. I was flying by VFR (visual flight rules), but I couldn't see anything. Between the violent winds and my disorientation, I lost control of the plane, and it began an uncontrollable dive toward the ground. An overwhelming feeling of helplessness threatened to paralyze me, but something began to rise up inside of me, and I began to shout it out: "I'm going to make it! I'm going to live! God, help me!"

Suddenly God began to speak inside of me about what to do. "Look at the instrument panel. Look at the instrument panel, and do what the instruments are telling you to do."

When you find yourself trapped in a storm of life, and you don't know what to do, don't be surprised when the voice of God says in your heart, "Look at My Word. Look at My Word, and say what I have spoken." God's Word is like a plane's instrument panel. When you believe and act in faith upon God's Word instead of your feelings, God can bring you out of the storm.

That day in the middle of the storm, I pulled my eyes away from the blank gray of the storm clouds in the windows of the cockpit and looked at the instrument panel before me. The airplane was being thrown around so violently that I couldn't tell if I was flying up, sideways, or upside down! I couldn't see anything because of the clouds.

> **K**eep your eyes on God's instrument panel for your life: the Word of God.

I felt as if I should do one thing, but the instrument panel told me to do something totally different! When I did what the instruments told me to do, the plane began to fly straight and level, and I came up out of that deadly dive before I hit the ground. If I had followed my human instincts and relied only on what my eyes and senses could tell me, I would have crashed and died that day. Instead, I obeyed God's direction and did what the instrument panel told me. Those instruments had access to information I did not have—they could see through the clouds and find true references about where the ground was. They could accurately tell me what was up and what was down. Once I followed the directions of God, I was able to escape tragedy, fly out of that stormy weather, and make it back home to my family.

Thank You, Jesus!

You may be in a storm right now, wondering, *What should I do? How do I come through?* Keep your eyes on God's instrument panel for your life: the Word of God. When you encounter any challenging situation, ask yourself, *What does God say about this?* His Word, the Bible, says: "And we know that all things work together for good to those who love God, to those who are the called according to His purpose" (Romans 8:28).

Once you decide to believe that God's Word is true and that you will make your decisions and guide your life according to His direction, then you must speak it out. You begin to say, "I will live and not die until my work in this world is finished, because that is God's promise. The Lord is my healer and deliverer."

God gets personally involved when we speak out His Word in faith! He told Jeremiah the prophet, "I am *watching over My word to perform it*" (Jeremiah 1:12, NASB, emphasis added).

From Death to Life...Twice!

THE STORY OF JOSE MIRANDA

The greatest joy of a parent's life is the birth of a child. I'll never forget the evening when my wife, Svetlana, gave birth to Sarah. Words can't express how I felt as a new father when we made handprints and footprints together for her pretend birth certificate.

Sarah was a very peaceful baby, but some of the nurses were concerned that she was too quiet. When she developed more serious symptoms, the doctors transferred her to the neonatal intensive care unit—but her condition only got worse.

Meanwhile, Svetlana began to have extreme headaches. We didn't think much of it, but then her pain increased over time and her back began to hurt.

Finally, my wife couldn't move her back or her neck. In tears, she said, "Sweetie, I don't feel good." Before I could even respond, Svetlana went into convulsions. The nurses rushed to get help, and within minutes an infectious disease specialist arrived.

He said Svetlana had bacterial meningitis, and he ordered a spinal tap for little Sarah that revealed she had viral meningitis! That was bad enough, but things were about to get worse.

A nurse told me, "Your wife is very sick, and she's probably not going to make it." Then a doctor said, "Mr. Miranda, we need to put your daughter in isolation. She has viral meningitis—and we have no medication or cure for that."

Suddenly, our joyful birth had turned into a potential double death scene for my young wife and my newborn daughter! There was little hope and no cure in sight.

What do you do in a situation like that? Then someone tried to "help" by saying, "I heard on the news that this mother and daughter had the same thing that your wife and daughter have. But they didn't make it." That just crushed me.

Harsh reality set in; I felt hopeless. *This could be it,* I thought. I couldn't understand why all of this was happening to me. I began to think: *Here I am, a good person in the ministry, loving on people. Why me? I am a giver and a tither. I'm a good person. Why me?*

Honestly, I felt God was abandoning me.

After fourteen days of antibiotics, Svetlana began to improve. Sarah, however, began to deteriorate. She couldn't open her eyes because she was so sedated, but her little head would turn every time I said, "Sarah, this is Daddy. I love you."

Our joyful birth had turned into a potential double death scene.

The doctors gave her medication to normalize her liver enzymes, but they warned that most children who receive it either hemorrhage (bleed) in the brain or become brain dead.

I looked at her little body—so bruised because of the IVs they had to insert and change so often. She looked like a little purple doll, and it just broke my heart.

Later, in Svetlana's room, I turned out the lights and waited until she fell asleep. Then I looked up into the pitch blackness of the room and said, "Lord, I can't control Svetlana or little Sarah, and I cannot control these doctors. But I can do something about me. I choose right now to believe You, and to make Your Word more real than the pain of this situation. Lord, I line up my life with Your Word. I don't understand it, and I don't know how to do it, so I trust You to help me through it. In the best way I know how, I believe my daughter is going to be fine. She's going to live and not die. And she's going to declare the works of the Lord."

The moment I chose to focus on God's Word and His goodness rather than on the bad things happening around me, I began to get strength. I saw things with a different perspective.

About ten days later, Svetlana and I got a call around midnight. "Mr. Miranda, you need to come right now because we don't think your daughter's going to make it through the night. Her heart is beginning to shut down... I think she has about an hour to live."

I immediately responded to the doctor with the words, "No, my daughter will live and not die; she will declare the works of the Lord."

The doctor said, "Excuse me, Mr. Miranda?" And I said once more: "My daughter is going to live and not die, and she's going to declare the works of the Lord."

Throughout the whole situation, the doctors kept telling us, "She's not going to make it. She may not make it, Mr. Miranda. We just want you to know that she's very ill."

We just came into agreement and spoke the Word of God over

her: "Sarah, you're going to live and not die, and you're going to declare the works of the Lord."

In just a matter of hours, the doctors came to us and said, "Your daughter has normalized." Then the heart specialist said, "Your daughter's heart is normal! It's like nothing ever happened to your daughter. You guys can go home."

I may not have all the answers when bad things happen to good people, but the one thing I do know is that I have a responsibility to trust the Word of God, to speak it out, and to trust the Lord to perform it.

I am grateful for the mercy of God. Because He is faithful, today I have my wife and daughter with me, and they are healthy and strong!

○ ○ ○ ○ ○

NEVER UNDERESTIMATE THE POWER OF YOUR WORDS!

"God said, 'Let there be light'; and there was light" (Genesis 1:3). God spoke, "Let the earth bear fruit" and it was so (see Genesis 1:11). The same God who spoke the world into being also said that your tongue (or power to speak) possesses the power of life and death. (After all, He created us in His own image and likeness—check out Genesis 1:26–27). It is like a fire, able to warm the hearts of millions or ignite a destructive firestorm that can destroy lives.

James said that if we think we are religious but fail to keep a tight rein on our tongues, then we are only deceiving ourselves—our religion is worthless (see James 1:26). Earlier we mentioned the role of the rudder on a large ship. Even that small rudder can steer a huge ship in the face of the strongest winds, if the rudder is in the hands of a skilled captain.

Something you say today may not seem to matter much to you, but it may have the power to accomplish nearly anything, or to destroy it!

Our words also have the awesome power to change the lives of those we love. We experienced this firsthand when our younger daughter, Ruth, went through a serious physical sickness when she was just a little baby. We took her to the doctor, and he accurately diagnosed her problem. But when he gave us the report, he delivered more than a set of clinical findings or lab results. As a strong Christian who happened to be a very skilled physician as well, he understood the power of the tongue. It was his duty to tell us the problem he had found, but he had another duty that was even higher: to remind us of the power of God. When this doctor shared the very discouraging diagnosis, he said, "Pastor Billy Joe and Sharon, this is her medical diagnosis, but by the stripes of Jesus, she is healed!"

Sharon and I understand the importance of spoken agreement in prayer and in matters of faith, so we immediately said, "We agree." Jesus said,

> Assuredly, I say to you, whatever you bind on earth will be bound in heaven, and whatever you loose on earth will be loosed in heaven.
>
> Again I say to you that if two of you agree on earth concerning anything that they ask, it will be done for them by My Father in heaven. For where two or three are gathered together in My name, I am there in the midst of them. (Matthew 18:18–20)

Notice that we didn't simply give silent mental assent—we said it and declared it out loud. Our daughter wasn't instantly healed that day. As with most healings, it took months for her healing to be completed. There are instantaneous miracles, and then there are times when a miracle happens over a period of time. Many people erroneously think that God hasn't heard their prayers or has refused to answer simply because an instantaneous miracle doesn't occur. In most healings, you must continue to exercise your faith and declare God's faithfulness with your mouth as the gradual healing process takes place. This is still a miracle, but on God's time line. We always need to trust God because He is faithful!

Ruth was totally healed in ten months! We knew it was a miracle. During the process we continued—without wavering—to speak God's Word over her life.

I encourage you to hold fast to the confession of your faith—without wavering, for the Lord who promised you is faithful to perform what He promised (see Hebrews 10:23).

That's God's Word.

NUGGETS FROM JESUS: THE POWER OF YOUR WORDS

One day Jesus and the disciples were walking toward Jerusalem, following a route over the Mount of Olives. He came to a fig tree that looked as if it would have figs, but it didn't (see Mark 11:13).

Then Jesus spoke these words to the tree: "Let no one eat fruit from you ever again" (v. 14).

The Bible doesn't say that anything dramatic happened at the time. Jesus and the disciples just went on into the city of Jerusalem. That was the day Jesus overturned the tables of the money-changers and the seats of the merchants who had set up shop inside the temple grounds as if it were a crafts bazaar (see vv. 15–18). Jesus and His disciples then left Jerusalem and walked back to Bethany, where they spent the night.

The next morning when they got up, Jesus led them along the same road toward Jerusalem. When they reached the fig tree, they noticed that it was withered from the root upward. The Bible says Peter remembered and said, "Rabbi, look! The fig tree which You cursed has withered away" (v. 21).

Then Jesus said, "Have faith in God" (v. 22).

What an amazing statement! Jesus was talking directly to them—and to us. What was this all about? Jesus had released His faith and spoken right in front of His disciples. Then they saw for themselves that exactly what He had said came to pass.

Finally, He let them know to release their faith: "For assuredly, I say to you, whoever says to this mountain, 'Be removed and be cast into the sea,' and does not doubt in his heart, but believes that those things he says will be done, he will have whatever he says. Therefore I say to you, whatever things you ask when you pray, believe that you receive them, and you will have them" (vv. 23–24).

How can I believe that what I declare is going to come to pass? I recommend that you speak what God's Word says, because we know that God watches over His Word to perform it! When you speak the Word of God, you know it is God's will, and you know He is waiting and willing to bring it to pass in every area of your life.

SEEING HOW GOD OPERATES

There are more than seven thousand promises in the Bible! Think of all of the truth, the commandments, the laws, and the statutes of God. Begin to speak them over your life so that God can bring them to pass.

Through His Word, God allows us to see how He operates. As we noted earlier, when God created the heavens and the earth in Genesis 1, the Bible tells us, "And God said." Those three words are repeated every time God created something and spoke something into existence.

Again, according to Genesis 1, you and I were made in the image and likeness of God (see vv. 26–27). He made it clear in His Word that

He also gave to us at least a faint measure of His creative power through the spoken word. You and I probably won't create planets and universes with our words, but God has given us authority in this world and in our lives.

Your words have power. That is why God made it a point to warn us in the Bible that "out of the abundance of the heart his mouth speaks" (Luke 6:45) and "death and life are in the power of the tongue" (Proverbs 18:21).

I urge you to apply this life-transforming message and redirect your life in the right way and in the right path. Now, from this day on, plant the eternal Word of God deeply into your heart and mind, and then speak it boldly in faith over your life, over your loved ones, and over your world!

One of the very best ways to begin is with the prayer Jesus taught us as His disciples to speak over our lives and the world:

Our Father which art in heaven, Hallowed be thy name.

Thy kingdom come, Thy will be done in earth, as it is in heaven.

Give us this day our daily bread.

And forgive us our debts, as we forgive our debtors.

And lead us not into temptation, but deliver us from evil:

For thine is the kingdom, and the power, and the glory, for ever. Amen. (Matthew 6:9–13, KJV)

5

Courage During Change and Uncertainty

Things are changing.

But **guess what?**

Not everything changes.

God does not **change,** and He says:

> No matter what, I'll always be with you. In the midst of sunny or stormy weather, I am with you. Whether the stock market is a bull or a bear, I am with you.
>
> Even when you lose someone you love, I am with you. So don't be sad. Be glad.

You're **not forgotten.**

You're **not forsaken.**

God is with you.

Through His Word, Jesus says to you and me, "Fear not."

Words like these were spoken throughout the Bible:

"Don't be afraid" (Matthew 17:7, NIV).

"Be of good courage" (Numbers 13:20).

"Be strong and courageous...for the LORD your God will be with you wherever you go" (Joshua 1:9, NIV). God is with you every step of the way—that is the key.

Jesus came to move inside your life, so you have no reason to fear. Your Guide, Protector, and Deliverer walks with you! He is your Provider, Savior, and Redeemer. He is your Peace, your Wisdom, your Joy, and your Life. Everything you need is provided in Him.

As we learn in Psalm 23, David discovered some incredible things about God during hard times:

The LORD is my shepherd;
   I shall not want.

He makes me to lie down in green pastures;
> He leads me beside the still waters.

He restores my soul;
> He leads me in the paths of righteousness
> For His name's sake.

Yea, though I walk through the valley of the shadow of death,
> I will fear no evil;
> For You are with me;
> Your rod and Your staff, they comfort me.

You prepare a table before me in the presence of my enemies;
> You anoint my head with oil;
> My cup runs over.

Surely goodness and mercy shall follow me
> All the days of my life;
> And I will dwell in the house of the LORD
> Forever.

This is God's promise to you too. If the Lord is your shepherd, then are you His sheep? Have you surrendered to Him? If you have, then fear has no place in your life. The Bible says, "For God has not given us a spirit of fear, but of power and of love and of a sound mind" (2 Timothy 1:7). Trust your heavenly Shepherd to lead you in the right places, provide you with what you need, and give you confidence to face every fear.

No matter what's going on in society, on Wall Street, or on Main Street—regardless of what crisis you face in your life, in the doctor's office, or at the office or plant—you can rise up and say, "Fear will have no place inside of me! The Lord is my shepherd. I know He is preparing a banquet table of blessings for me to enjoy right in front of my enemies!" When you think about David's situation when he wrote Psalm 23, he certainly was not talking about a future banquet in heaven, because there will be no enemies there! David was speaking about victory celebrations the Lord sets up for us on earth. God delights to bless those who trust Him, and He often does it openly and publicly, right in front of the Enemy and even in front of the people in our lives who wrongly accuse or oppose us.

> God delights to bless those
> who trust Him.

As you follow the Good Shepherd, He will anoint you with the oil of His Spirit, pour His Holy Spirit upon you, and cause the cup of your life to overflow with His blessings! And it will be a big "I told you so!" in the face of the devil.

When Sharon and I were first married, we lived in a $65-a-month apartment (all utility bills and bugs included). At the time I read a book about how to get ready for the "disastrous calamities and tragedies" that the author believed were imminent. I was young in the Lord, so that book created fear in my life because I didn't have enough foundation in God's Word.

One thing the author suggested was that anyone who wanted to survive those times should pick up nuts in nearby wooded areas and store them as food. I told Sharon, "Now we've got to get ready. We've got to get prepared." So off we went to a local park where we loaded up grocery bags with acorns we found on the ground. Then we took them home like a pair of satisfied squirrels, all prepared for winter. Once we had carried our gathered treasure into the apartment, I said, "Well, Sharon, let's roast a few of these acorns and eat some so we'll know what it's going to be like." We picked out some good-looking candidates and carefully heated them up. After one bite, I had a revelation and a declaration: "God, You have something better for us than acorns!" The dire events and terrible tragedies that author predicted in his book never did come to pass, and that was many years ago! Yet at that time, the fear in me was so real that it gripped my soul.

You may know exactly how it feels to feel pressured or even terrorized by things that you've read or heard. I encourage you to go back to the Good Book—the good news—and read what God says about providing for His people in times of famine. King David said:

> I have been young, and now am old;
> > Yet I have not seen the righteous forsaken,
> > Nor his descendants begging bread. (Psalm 37:25)

I know that things turned around for us when we read the promises in God's Word and declared together, "Lord, we believe that You will make a way."

I believe it will happen in your life too. Let go of fear and take hold of faith! Again, God has not given you a spirit of fear, but of power, love, and a sound mind. Fear is a spirit, and God has given you a different spirit—the Spirit of power. According to the apostle Paul, it is "the Spirit of Him who raised Jesus from the dead"! And that Spirit—the Holy Spirit—dwells in you! Romans 8:10–11 reads, "And if Christ is in you, the body is dead because of sin, but the Spirit is life because of righteousness. But if the Spirit of Him who raised Jesus from the dead dwells in you, He who raised Christ from the dead will also give life to your mortal bodies through His Spirit who *dwells in you*" (emphasis added).

God also poured His spirit of love into your heart. This is not just God's love for you but also God's love flowing through you!

He also gave you the spirit of a sound mind. You were not born to be tormented, confused, or harassed in your thinking. The Lord's gift of the spirit of a sound mind reflects His thoughts and plans for you.

"For I know the plans that I have for you," declares the LORD,
"plans for welfare and not for calamity to give you a future and a hope." (Jeremiah 29:11, NASB)

Your thoughts are to be clear, accurate, and on target. That will never happen if you let fear rule your life. When you came into God's family through Jesus, He exchanged any old fears you had with His gift—the spirit of power, love, and a sound mind in your life.

GREAT TIME FOR A MENTAL BREAKDOWN?

Think about the moment when Moses' "great escape parade" came to an abrupt halt at the shores of the Red Sea with six hundred thousand men (along with their families and livestock) behind him wondering what was going on.

And then there was Pharaoh and the armies of Egypt right behind them in hot and angry pursuit. Talk about emotional stress! You may feel that way today. Perhaps you have impossible problems behind you and an impassable problem in front of you. You are surrounded by unpleasant issues with no place to run. Moses would understand. He had more than a million critics behind him. (And they were all complaining and criticizing him at full volume.) I can only imagine what they were asking Moses:

"Why did you do this?"

"What were you thinking?"

"Now explain to us again just why you brought us here?"

Meanwhile, Moses was staring at the Red Sea knowing that if he tried to swim across that sea, almost every Israelite behind him would drown. If he turned around, then Pharaoh and his army were waiting to kill him and return the children of Israel to slavery. There appeared to be no way out. And that is when Moses shouted to the fearful followers around him, "Fear ye not, stand still, and see the salvation of the LORD" (Exodus 14:13, KJV). Then he boldly declared that the Lord would fight for them if they would be quiet!

In that moment when you are surrounded by the impossible and hounded by your fears about finances, family, a job situation, or serious issues in your own life—that is the ideal time to stand up on the inside by faith and say, "The Lord is going to fight for us. He's going to deliver us. He's going to make a way for us!"

Boxers call wild swings at an opponent "haymakers." But God has delivered some "waymakers" for you that can deliver precise and powerful punches to level the obstacles and problems you face today.

- The psalmist said: "The LORD is my light and my salvation; whom shall I fear?" (Psalm 27:1).
- Jesus said: "In the world you will have tribulation; but be of good cheer, I have overcome the world" (John 16:33).
- Paul put it this way: "If God is for us, who can be against us?" (Romans 8:31).
- And John said: "For whatever is born of God overcomes the world. And this is the victory that has overcome the world— our faith. Who is he who overcomes the world, but he who believes that Jesus is the Son of God" (1 John 5:4–5).

Jesus gave you His overcoming power, and your faith is the key to releasing it. John told us that faith is the victory that overcomes the world. Are you wondering, *How do I get through this mess?* Just remember this: faith is the key.

Someone said, "Fear knocked at the door. Faith answered, and no one was there." You may wonder why I talk about faith so much and what faith has to do with your life. Let me put it this way, you have a choice: you can either walk by faith or be driven by fear.

> **R**efuse to allow fear to rule your life.

Only God knows how may people at this very moment are being tormented, bound, driven, oppressed, and pushed down because they don't know how to deal with the spirit of fear!

On the other hand, the people who choose to walk by faith are victorious and full of joy. You can live under the bondage of fear…or you can live as an overcomer through Christ!

People living in fear and people living by faith face exactly the same circumstances, but their responses, attitudes, and spirits are quite different. And they produce radically different results. That is because fear and faith work the same way, but in opposite directions! They both hear, they both believe, they both speak, and they both act.

When people hear bad things they begin to believe them, speak them, and act upon them. Evidently, fear, doubt, and unbelief come by hearing the voices of the world. The Bible says that faith comes by hearing God's Word (see Romans 10:17). You believe, speak, and act upon the words you hear and receive. Fear takes you into the curse; faith takes you to the blessing.

I encourage you to choose faith over fear today. Refuse to allow fear to rule your life. Choose to walk by faith in God's Word and not merely by what you see (see 2 Corinthians 5:17).

"I'm a Trophy of God's Mercy"

THE RESTORATION OF CARMEN GIL

When you grow up with no father or mother, you grow up with an emptiness in your soul. As a child in Bolivia, I used to watch people nurture their children and give them a kiss or a hug. And I wondered, *How does it feel to be loved with such a love?*

I dreamed that one day I would marry and have children who would know how it felt to have a home with a mother and a father. They would have the refrigerator full of food and never know what it is to be hungry and cold, because I would provide for them.

When I came to the United States, I thought, *My whole life will change because now I am in the land of endless opportunity!*

I married a young man from Venezuela who was studying to become an engineer, and we had two children before he was called back home under a rigid three-year work agreement with his company.

He grew to like living in Venezuela, apart from me and the children. When he finally returned to the United States, he demanded a divorce despite my pleas and arguments to keep the family together.

The tragedy that I wanted to avoid so much had happened to me. *If God really existed,* I reasoned, *then why did this happen to me and my children?*

Three years later I met a man from my country, Bolivia, and began to think that he was "the right person" I had always needed. After all, he was from my country, and we smoked the same cigarettes, drank the same liquor, and sang the same songs. Finally, I thought, I can make life work for me.

We married and he loved my children. I was very happy for a time. We bought a new car, and I thought I was building my American dream once again.

Then my second husband said, "Honey, I got to go back to Bolivia. My mother is dying, and the family says I have to come right now." We gathered the money for his two-week emergency visit to Bolivia and put him on the plane.

One morning I woke up and said, "Hey, God, will You please kill me?"

Two weeks later, he called from Bolivia to say, "I'm sorry, I will not be returning to Tulsa. I didn't realize that my passport and visa had both expired. They won't ever let me come back to the United States again."

This was the second time life had stolen everything I had! I began to scream, cry, and kick the walls of my home—uncontrollably in my anger at life.

That day I was driving in the car with my sister when I had to hit the brakes and the car went into an uncontrolled spin and finally crashed. At the hospital, the doctor announced that I didn't have any broken bones, but there was one large surprise—I was pregnant.

I wasn't so happy about this. Now I would have three children to raise without a father. I already knew how it felt to go through a divorce, but now I faced an even greater fear. It gripped my heart to the point that I could scarcely breathe.

One morning I woke up and said, "Hey, God, will You please kill me? Do me a favor and just kill me. I have too much pain and I've lost everything. I have no dreams, and I don't want to live. Just kill me, please?" That was my first prayer.

It was clear after a few minutes that I was still alive, so I made a second request: "God, will You please show me somehow, somewhere, that You are real?"

Then I clearly heard a voice say, *God loves you and He died for you. He loves you more than your first husband, and more than your second husband.* And finally I heard the voice say, *I didn't just give you forgiveness of sin. I want to give you a restoration—so you will know that with Me you will not lack anything.*

My faith in the Lord grew much stronger as I discovered that the beautiful God I was beginning to know could not only speak to my heart and comfort me in my lonely times, but He could also provide for me and my family.

Single parents like me seem to deal with a lot of guilt because we have to leave our children to go to work. When we finally get back home, we are tired and we often go to sleep thinking we are the most horrible parents in the world because we don't get to spend enough time with our children.

I've learned that God takes care of us and provides for our needs. He will even restore and redeem the things seemingly lost through all the mistakes that we make!

I am a trophy of His mercy. He's big enough to conquer your fears, conquer your depression, and to be a father for the fatherless! He is big enough to make all your dreams come to pass.

○ ○ ○ ○ ○

FAITH WILL CARRY YOU THROUGH LIFE'S STORMS

Where is your faith in the middle of the storm? Let's take a look at one of the great incidents told in the New Testament (see Mark 4:36–41).

Luke, the physician and disciple of Jesus, described the day the Lord and all of the disciples boarded a ship to cross the Sea of Galilee. Jesus went to sleep in the boat, and when a violent storm suddenly arose, the disciples began to cry out in fear: "Master, don't You care that we're gonna drown?" (see v. 38).

It was a horrible moment: fear gripped the twelve disciples and put them into a panic just when they needed faith and unity so desperately. Frankly, many of us today secretly wonder how these men could possibly have forgotten that Jesus was right there with them!

Finally, Jesus stood up in the boat and spoke directly to the wind and to the water with the command: "Peace, be still" (v. 39). Immediately the wind and the sea became calm, and Jesus turned to His disciples to ask, "Why are you so fearful? How is it that you have no faith?" (v. 40).

The disciples were stunned. What was He talking about? Evidently Jesus expected them to deal with the storm themselves, or at the very least, to deal with their fear in the midst of the storm.

You may be in the middle of a storm and right now are wondering, *Is Jesus sleeping? Doesn't He care that I'm going under here? We're out of money, out of hope, and out of faith. I guess this is it.*

No, Jesus is alive forevermore! He is seated at the right hand of the Father at this moment, and He has already defeated death, hell, and the grave. *He has given you His victory.* Jesus isn't asleep—He's waiting on you! There is power dwelling within you, so it is time to stand up and rebuke those things that are trying to torment and bind your life. God didn't give you that spirit of fear, so drop it! Now stand up and, in the name of Jesus, command peace to your situation, because you have been given the spirit of power, love, and a sound mind.

The Lord is your shepherd, so you don't have to be afraid. He sticks with you even if you are walking through the valley of the shadow of death! He is there when attacks are coming against you from every side.

Now you can shout with King David and the apostle Paul, "The Lord is my light and He's my salvation. Whom shall I fear? If the Lord is on my side, then who can be against me?"

Your God causes, "all things [to] work together for good" (Romans 8:28). He dwells inside of you, and He is greater than he that is in the world. Release the truth to set you free from fear forever. This is the day to let the truth from God's Word empower you to walk in victory in every area. The truth will carry you through every situation that you may face where you are confronted by fear.

> **T**his is the day to let the truth from God's Word empower you
> to walk in victory in every area.

One time we took a missions trip to the Republic of Sierra Leone in West Africa during a long and bloody war. First we flew to the city of Bo, the nation's second-largest city, only about fifty miles from where the rebels were based. I remember flying over the region and thinking, *Do those rebels have missiles? Can they hit us where we are—in this helicopter?* In spite of the danger, we had a strong sense of calm and peace. We were in the exact place where God had called us to be.

During our first meeting that night, God opened the blind eyes of a little boy and touched the city. In fact, the miracle had such a powerful impact that the Muslim imam (the leader of the Muslims in that city) announced every day on his loudspeaker during the five daily calls to prayer: "If you need healing, go to the crusade fields." As a result, thousands of people came to Christ!

Then we entered Freetown, the national capital and largest city, to conduct a crusade in the national soccer stadium. God spoke to me in the middle of our service to have one of the former rebel leaders who had been born again lead everyone in declaring, "Jesus is Lord!" The people shouted continuously at the top of their voices for about fifteen minutes, declaring to the heavens and to their nation, "Jesus is Lord over Sierra Leone!"

Only a few weeks after that bold faith declaration, the rebels laid down their weapons…after eleven years of war. Without a single major battle or another drop of blood being shed, those Christians waged war in the heavenlies and overcame the spiritual forces that had terrorized their country and killed or maimed thousands of people!

Fear will keep you from doing things that will help others. But when you conquer fear with the truth of God's Word, then you will walk in the power and blessings of God.

6

Hearing
God's Voice

What does **your life** sound like?

- phones ringing in your office and home
- a dog barking (at everything)
- thunder, rain, and wind of a storm
- a baby crying (over a wet diaper, hunger, or seeking comfort because of colic)
- car horns (from an impatient spouse or hundreds of drivers in rush hour)
- muffled evidence of endless traffic passing by your office window
- sirens that startle you in the night or shatter your day
- a blaring television that has become a forgotten soundtrack to your routine
- the crack of a bat, a ref's shrill whistle, and a crowd's roar in a crowded gym
- the door bell (after the boy next door discovered how it works)

the murmur of a crowd before a play or at a party
shock waves from broken glass
hammering, shouted directions, and heavy machinery
of construction
the chatter of children in a crowded waiting room
the layered battle of voices as you search for a radio
station

What does God **sound** like?
With so much noise, how would you know?
We live in a big, loud world.
God speaks in a still, small voice.

So take a **moment.**

Unplug.
Press the mute button.
Step off the roller coaster.

God is **speaking.** Are you **listening**?

We should *all* expect to hear God's voice. After all, He is our loving Father and we are His children. Loving parents talk to their children, and their children speak back to them. There is a natural exchange between people in such a close relationship.

You probably know you can talk to God in prayer. But do you think that God might want to speak to you?

How would He speak? you wonder.

God has been known to speak audibly, or out loud, to people throughout history. He has not lost His voice. He spoke directly to Adam in the garden, and He also gave Noah specific verbal instructions about building the ark. He told Abraham to leave the place where he was and go to a land that He would show him. He also spoke to Isaac and Jacob, the son and grandson of Abraham. In each case God delivered specific instructions to these people—instructions that were recorded in the Bible.

Most people today don't hear God speak because they simply don't expect to hear, or they don't *want* to hear! But God speaks in many ways. While He speaks audibly in some cases, He *constantly* communicates to us through His Word, the Bible. He also speaks through His prophets, as seen in the book of Acts and 1 Corinthians 12 and 14. Sometimes God speaks through circumstances, such as when doors supernaturally open and close. This happened to the apostle Paul when he wanted to evangelize Asia Minor. He had the direction right, but apparently he was unclear on God's timing. On two different occasions the Holy Spirit directly intervened to stop the apostle from going to the region before God's appointed time (see Acts 16:6–10).

The Lord also speaks through anointed leaders, teachers, and counselors who give counsel, instructions, and training based on His Word. Others offer unique insight that is anointed and confirmed by the Holy Spirit. In the New Testament this happened when James the Lesser stood up after hours of discussion in a crucial meeting in Jerusalem and *declared the final direction* on a major doctrinal matter (see Acts 15, especially vv. 13–19).

God also speaks directly to your inner man through the inner witness of the Holy Spirit, who gives you a deep sense of peace (a divine "yes"), or a deep sense of unrest over a decision or question (a divine "no"), as described in Colossians 3.

There are many other ways that God speaks as well. That is why Jesus said, "If anyone has ears to hear, let him hear" (Mark 4:23). I'm positive that most of us have ears on the side of our heads, but the majority of human beings are not following Jesus at this moment. So what was the Lord talking about? I think He was referring to our willingness and our commitment to *listening*. We must be open, attentive, and receptive to hear the voice of God.

You may be thinking, *Oh, that "talking to God and our hearing Him" business is only for a few folks.* I urge you to rethink that thought. The Bible, from the front cover to the back, recounts the many times that God spoke and people listened! Those people who listened and acted upon what God said were delivered from disaster, cruel plots, invasion, disease, and tragedies of all kinds.

> **W**e must be open, attentive, and receptive to hear the voice of God.

If you are still breathing and even slightly aware of current events in the world, then you *know* it is time for people everywhere to listen to God! If you have moved and you urgently need to find and purchase a house right now, wouldn't it be wonderful to *hear God's counsel* on what house to buy? Perhaps you want to find an apartment, but you don't know what apartment complex is best for your family and your personal safety. Wouldn't you like to have two minutes with God to seek His advice? Wouldn't it be great to know *where to invest your money* at the moment?

Many years ago, I heard God tell me, *Get your money out of that bank.* Sharon and I had only been married for a few years and only managed to save $2,000 or $3,000. To us, that was a whole lot of money, so I was very surprised when God said to me, *Get your money out of that bank.*

Just for reassurance, I asked a friend of mine who had a solid understanding of business and was involved with the business community, "Is there anything wrong with this bank?"

"No," he said "everything is on the up and up. It's doing well."

"Okay," I said and let it go.

Then that voice came back: "Get your money out of that bank." That was enough for me. I went down and withdrew our money from that particular bank so that I could transfer it into another bank.

Sharon asked me, "What are you doing?" And I said, "Well, all I know is I heard the Lord say we were to get our money out of that bank." She understood and immediately accepted the decision.

I'll never forget opening the newspaper just a few weeks later. A large picture sprawled across the front page showed some desperate people banging on the doors of that bank! At 5:00 p.m. on the previous afternoon, the directors had locked the bank and announced that it had been shut down by federal bank regulators.

Many people would say, "Well, at least those people had their money insured." But are you aware of how long it takes for the Federal Deposit Insurance Corporation (FDIC) to process a bank closure? Regulators have to go through every bank record to verify that you had money in the bank in the first place. Then it takes even longer to deliver the reimbursement to you! Some folks struggle for *months* while waiting to receive their money!

I thought about it that day and asked the Lord, *God, did You just speak to me? Or were You speaking to others as well?*

Today, I know that God loves everybody. That means He also talks to—or *wants* to talk to—everyone. The Bible assures us that "there is no partiality with God" (Romans 2:11), which means we have to listen, and we have to remain open and receptive to His voice. Remember: He can make a way where there seems to be no way *if we'll listen.* Open your heart and let God speak to you.

HAVE YOU SENSED GOD SPEAKING...TO YOU?

God has not lost His voice.

He's still speaking.

He loves you, so He is going to speak to you.

He will reveal the plans He has for you if you open yourself to hear

His voice. In fact, Jesus spoke to seven complete *churches* in Revelation 2 and 3. What do you think He said *seven times,* once after the individual message He delivered to each church? "He who has an ear, let him hear what the Spirit says to the churches" (Revelation 2:7). He said this to all seven churches, and it still rings true for you and me today: *If you have the ability to hear God, then listen up!*

I'm convinced that God speaks in one way or another to everyone. But many have not recognized His voice or simply haven't been open to receiving from Him. This often happens when people have already determined their own direction.

Sometimes God speaks to us to deliver us from a crisis or from captivity. At other times He speaks to help us walk out His purposes. He may speak specific directions to help you touch the people He has assigned to you. It is clear that He spoke to people all the way through the Bible. Don't say, "Well, that was *then.* This is *now.*" The Bible already has an unshakable answer to that excuse: "Jesus Christ is the same yesterday, today, and forever" (Hebrews 13:8). God still speaks, and He doesn't change.

"SPEAK. I'M YOUR SERVANT, READY TO LISTEN"

A lot of people have something in common with the young boy Samuel: they don't realize God is speaking to them. Here's how that story unfolded:

> The boy Samuel was serving GOD under Eli's direction. This was at a time when the revelation of GOD was rarely heard or seen. One night Eli was sound asleep…. It was well before dawn; the sanctuary lamp was still burning. Samuel was still in bed in the Temple of GOD, where the Chest of God rested.
>
> Then GOD called out, "Samuel, Samuel!"

Samuel answered, "Yes? I'm here." Then he ran to Eli saying, "I heard you call. Here I am."

Eli said, "I didn't call you. Go back to bed." And so he did.

GOD called again, "Samuel, Samuel!"

Samuel got up and went to Eli, "I heard you call. Here I am."

Again Eli said, "Son, I didn't call you. Go back to bed." (This all happened before Samuel knew GOD for himself. It was before the revelation of GOD had been given to him personally.)

GOD called again, "Samuel!"—the third time! Yet again Samuel got up and went to Eli. "Yes? I heard you call me. Here I am."

That's when it dawned on Eli that GOD was calling the boy. So Eli directed Samuel, "Go back and lie down. If the voice calls again, say, 'Speak, GOD. I'm your servant, ready to listen.'" Samuel returned to his bed.

Then GOD came and stood before him exactly as before, calling out, "Samuel! Samuel!"

Samuel answered, "Speak. I'm your servant, ready to listen." (1 Samuel 3:1–10, MSG)

Three times Samuel ran in to check with Eli the priest (who didn't have a clue about what was going on). Finally Eli realized what was happening and said, "Samuel, it's the Lord speaking to you."

The next time God called young Samuel, he said, "Speak, Lord, for Your servant is listening." Then, in the first of countless supernatural communications, God revealed what He was about to do in the land of Israel.

The Lord will reveal future things to us too. In fact, God's Word specifically says that the Holy Spirit will show us things to come (see John 16:13). We met a man whose son experienced this firsthand.

One day right in the middle of an altar call at the end of a service, a man ran down the stairs and headed directly for the platform. Since I was focused on praying for people at the time, I directed him to my wife and he spoke to her. As soon as I was finished praying with other people, Sharon told me, "You need to hear what this man has to say."

A commercial jetliner had recently crashed in the Everglades, killing everyone on board. This man said he knew his son was scheduled to be on that flight. He and his wife sat glued to the television for hours, praying. Before their son left, they had already prayed and believed for him to be protected, delivered, and kept safe. Nevertheless, they didn't hear a word about *anyone's having survived* that crash, and the hours since the crash were mounting.

It seems that just before takeoff, the young man already had his bags loaded and was about to walk down the entryway onto the plane when he heard the Lord say, *Don't get on that plane.*

He told the stewardess, "My friend and I have got to get off." Then this young man and his friend drove to another airport nearby to catch a later flight going up the coast. That is why his parents didn't hear from him right away.

When the young man arrived at his parents' home, he told them he had taken a different flight. So the grateful father who ran down the steps that day at our service had come to tell us what had happened. His son is alive today *because he heard—and heeded—God's voice*!

Your ability to hear God's voice could be the difference between life and death, between blessing and cursing, or between your arrival in the right place or finding yourself in the wrong place at the wrong time! You may think this topic is boring, but I'm telling you, it's the number one thing to pay attention to after you receive Jesus Christ! You must be ready and open to hear the voice of God on every occasion! Remember, your God loves you and cares about you. He has people that you need in your life, along with key places and vital jobs for you to do.

Remember, if you hear His voice—
You can be at the right place,
at the right time
doing the right thing
with the right people in the right way.

Reaching Millions in the USSR

TOM NEWMAN'S STORY

I've had the heart of an evangelist ever since I became a Christian. An evangelist goes where the people are. The tool or method I believe God gave me to "go to the people" is the medium of performance.

Early in 1986, I was touring with *A Toymaker's Dream* as producer and performer. It is a dramatic dance allegory of the gospel that uses a combination of professional lighting, special effects, costuming, and dance to communicate what I believe is the most powerful message on this planet—the love story between God, His people, and His Son.

We pulled into the parking lot of Rock Church in Virginia Beach, Virginia, and parked our bus underneath this large sign that says, "Jesus is Lord over Rock Church."

When I looked at that, I just felt grieved in my heart. Rock Church wasn't the problem—that's a great church. I just felt a sense of, *I don't want to entertain Christians—I want to reach this generation.*

As soon as I got the words out of my mouth, I had this *overwhelming knowing.* I sensed God saying, *Tom, I want you to go to the Soviet Union.*

Today that may not seem like such a big deal, but just a few years earlier, President Ronald Reagan had called the Soviet Union an "evil empire"—so my mind was immediately flooded with negative thoughts: *You can't go to the Soviet Union! How do you even get into the Soviet Union? Nobody goes there. You especially don't go into the Soviet Union and preach or proclaim the gospel!*

Then I started to add to the list with my own questions and comments. *I don't know anybody in the Soviet Union... Where do I begin?*

Then I heard that musician and songwriter Billy Joel had just completed a big tour there as part of a cultural exchange program with the United States Information Agency (USIA). So I contacted the agency to see how I could apply for a tour.

I received a stack of forms and filled out pages and pages of material. About two months later, I received a letter that said, "Congratulations, your material has been accepted. You are one of eighteen hundred groups qualified to participate in our cultural exchange program with the USSR."

Then I asked, "How many teams go over there each year?" It turned out that only two to three groups a year actually went! So I asked a second question: "Is there any way that we could kind of jump ahead on the list?"

They said, "Well, you can always go over with us when we make the presentations to potential host cities." That was all I needed to know.

First we went to a place called Tashkent. They weren't interested, so we went to Kiev, and they weren't interested either. The same thing happened in Leningrad (now called St. Petersburg) and Moscow.

We went to several different places in Moscow to make presentations, but no one expressed any interest. One day I went downstairs to a restaurant in our hotel. I sat down and literally put my hand on my head and started a conversation with the Lord.

"God, I know when I was at Rock Church, You said, 'Go to the Soviet Union.' So I'm here. And I don't know what else to do. I really, really, *really* want to be responsive and do what You've asked of me, but I don't have any answers." And that is when I looked up.

When God speaks, He can move all of heaven and all of earth.

A guy was walking across the restaurant toward me. There were only four people in this restaurant built to seat a thousand, and this guy was making a beeline right toward me!

At the time I had long hair and a beard because I was playing the part of Jesus in *A Toymaker's Dream*. This man walked right up to me, put his hands on the table, and leaned in to look into my eyes. Then he said, "Are you a rock'n'roll musician?"

"Well, kind of."

"Okay, why are you here?"

I took a deep breath and said, "Well, we have a dramatic dance presentation that we would like to bring into this country. We're holding meetings and searching for someone who would be interested in having us come over here."

He nodded and said, "Here's my card." Then he added, "You give this to taxi man and have him bring you to my place in an hour and a half. I'll take care of everything."

I shrugged and said, "Okay."

In ninety minutes, the man somehow gathered together the heads of the Soviet Peace Committee and the Young Communist Party, and the people from Gos Concert, the organization that had brought in Billy Joel that year. Once I was in front of them, he said, "Okay, show them your stuff."

So I plugged in our little promo videotape with its Russian voice track. They watched it and said, "Very nice, we're going to sign you up." Before I knew it, everybody was all but high-fiving, and we were writing in the dates for a six-week tour.

By the time we left the Soviet Union in 1989, we had completed two tours with the *Toymaker* team, reaching hundreds of thousands of people in live performances and potentially touching millions with the gospel through live television broadcasts.

It was an amazing thing. When God speaks, He can move all of heaven and all of earth.

○ ○ ○ ○ ○

LEARN TO HEAR HIS STILL, SMALL VOICE

Communication is vital. As God's ambassadors and messengers on earth, it is important to search out every possible way to spread the good news of Jesus and the Cross using television, radio, the Internet, iPods, and the ever-growing social networking media. Why? If we want to reach *people,* then we need to get the message out by using the language and media that people actually use!

God has the greatest message of all! And He speaks through countless ways in virtually endless creativity. For instance, we know He speaks through the written and spoken Word, but He *also* speaks through dreams, visions, and signs and wonders. These are simply components of God's audiovisual department.

And every time He speaks—regardless of the particular form or method He uses—He always speaks directly to our hearts and into our lives.

Just think of the creative way God spoke to Mary (the teenager who became the mother of Jesus). Now think about how God delivered His messages to Abraham, Isaac, Jacob, Daniel, Joseph, and the apostle Paul—just to name a few! People heard God speaking *throughout* the Bible. On the day he baptized Jesus at the Jordan River, John the Baptist heard God's voice say, "This is My beloved Son, in whom I am well pleased" (Matthew 3:17). Much later, Peter, James, and John heard God speak the same words about Jesus while they were on the Mount of Transfiguration (see Matthew 17:5).

He is speaking to *you* today. His voice is clear and He has plans for you. He also has definite directions to help you carry them out. As you hear and obey, you will walk in a place of blessing! But don't get caught up worrying about *how* He will speak. Let God handle that department. He will speak in whatever way is needed to *reach you*!

Elijah was one of the greater Old Testament prophets—I'm sure you've read about him in 1 Kings 18 and 19. He called down fire from heaven and defeated hundreds of pagan prophets, but then he was intimidated by a wicked queen named Jezebel. The crisis so unsettled Elijah that he doubted his ability to hear God, as well as God's ability to protect him. He ran in fear and hid in the wilderness, thinking God had deserted him and that he was the only believer left alive.

God spoke to him, but first He taught this prophet *not to put Him in a box.* God sent along a strong wind, a violent storm, then an earthquake, and finally a fire. Yet His voice wasn't contained in any of those things. God spoke to his disheartened prophet in a "still small voice" (1 Kings 19:12). It is a still voice because everything else fades away when God speaks.

The Lord didn't have to shout at Elijah, and He doesn't have to shout at you either! Yet, however He speaks to you, it will be with divine authority and clarity. Trust God. He will see to it that you successfully hear His voice and receive divine direction.

Much like my friend Tom Newman, I have a story concerning God's direction to go to Russia. When God asked us to go to Russia, it wasn't to be a single trip. He told us to go back every month for eighteen months in a row!

We had managed to hold a crusade in a huge indoor stadium in St. Petersburg, Russia. While we were there, God spoke to me and said, "Go back. These people need the Word of the Lord."

I had forgotten that back in 1980 a woman had prophesied: "The door to Russia will open in the days ahead, and the gospel will be preached from one end to the other, and there will be people that will sweep across that nation and reap the end-times harvest."

At that time, God spoke to me and said I would be one of those people. This woman turned and spoke the exact statement to me. Eleven years had passed since that word had been given.

When God spoke to me in St. Petersburg, the original prophetic word from 1980 dropped into my spirit once more. We were supposed to be there, but by that time we had already closed the crusade and were en route home.

> In every plan and timetable, God still needs someone "with ears to hear."

Once we got back to Tulsa, we attempted to go back and get people to help us. Russia was in the midst of unprecedented change—which was accompanied by turmoil and fear. It seemed that none of the people we had met in Russia wanted to do another crusade and outreach—particularly since we had been there just three months earlier in November 1991. However, when God speaks to you, you can't let go of it. I kept hearing Him say, "Go, go." Finally one Sunday morning before church, I told Sharon, "We're going to Russia. *Someone* will come."

After the Sunday service that morning, three people walked up to me—I had never seen or spoken to any of them before. They had never written or called us either. They said in a thick accent: "We hear you're going to Russia. We want to help you."

I said, "Who are you?" After they gave me their names, I asked, "Where are you from?"

"We are from St. Petersburg," they said, and they explained they had heard that I had told our people we were going. They were exactly what we needed.

In our first crusade, more than twenty-five thousand people made signed decisions for Christ. When we went back in January, more than ninety thousand people received Jesus Christ as Lord. And each month we returned for eighteen consecutive months, more and more Russians came to Jesus. It was like an avalanche.

God had a plan and a time then, and He has a plan and a time for your life too. In every plan and timetable, God still needs someone with ears to hear. You may struggle with it just as I did, and in the same way Tom Newman and the young man who was about to board the deadly flight struggled with God's divine messages. Let me encourage you—the struggle to hear and obey is *always* worth it. In the end, we will *all* be thankful that we *listened* when God spoke and by grace obeyed Him!

Will you dare to listen for and obey God's voice? Perhaps you will be the one obedient servant God uses to birth a mighty move in your city or nation! Whatever happens in God's kingdom in the days ahead, without a doubt it will begin with God speaking and with His people *listening*.

Do you have ears to hear?

7

What God
Thinks of You

Who do you **think** you are?

No, really—**who?**
    brother
    daughter
    mom
    Mr. Mom
    graduate
    athlete
    ex-husband
    surgeon
    tree-hugger
    African
    Asian
    Caucasian
    Hispanic

Who do **others** think you are?
    life of the party
    backseat driver
    black sheep
    teacher
    friend
    housewife

desperate housewife
overachiever
over the hill
the tooth fairy
Santa Claus

Ever considered who God thinks you are? (After all, **He made you!**) He says you are:
loved
wanted
chosen
beautiful
on purpose
for a purpose
unique
wonderfully made
justified
irreplaceable
worth it

You are **valuable.**

God thinks you're **important,** His very special treasure.

God cares about you. He knows all about you, and He loves you, not because of what you've done or because of your awards and accomplishments. He loves you simply because He made you.

I'm convinced that every time God looks at you or thinks about you (which is constantly), He sees a likeness and image of Himself! In fact, He said that He made you—and every other human being—using Himself as a model (see Genesis 1:26–27).

He values you as you are and right where you are. As we learned earlier, God really does think about you. He said, "For I know *the thoughts that I think toward you,* says the LORD, thoughts of peace and not of evil, to give you a future and a hope" (Jeremiah 29:11, emphasis added).

I want to ask you a question… Just how valuable are you?

I won't be surprised to see you pull out your official statement of net worth if you are a certified public accountant or a businessperson, but that isn't what I'm asking! Your true worth simply cannot be calculated on a mathematical basis. If it could be, then perhaps you could add to your net financial worth the $4.50 that the U.S. Bureau of Chemistry and

Soils says approximates the total worth of your physical body when reduced to its base components of carbon, mineral traces, and metals. (This includes the $3.50 net value of your skin based on a value of 25¢ per square foot.)

Don't get depressed yet. Many things cannot be valued solely on the basis of numbers and chemical analysis.

Both a lump of coal and the celebrated Hope Diamond share one basic and common quality—they are both composed of carbon, one of the most common substances on our planet. Yet most of us would have a clear preference for the Hope Diamond, owned and displayed by the Smithsonian Natural History Museum and estimated to be worth $300 million to $350 million! The truth is that your worth cannot be quantified, or reduced, to a number. In fact, every measure of worth involves comparisons to other things considered valuable by most people, nations, and authorities. In God's eyes, you are worth more than all of the earthly things we consider valuable—that means all of the discovered and undiscovered gold, silver, and precious stones on earth.

> **R**elax. God didn't send Jesus only for perfect
> people, because there are none.

Jesus said, "For God so loved the world that he gave his one and only Son, that whoever believes in him shall not perish but have eternal life" (John 3:16, NIV).

Relax. God didn't send Jesus only for perfect people, because there are none. He didn't come for only one type of people—because He made all of us and He doesn't play favorites (see Romans 2:11, NIV)! It doesn't matter to Him whether you are rich or poor, tall or short, smart or not so smart, male or female, young or old. No matter what color your skin may be or what language you speak, Jesus Christ came to lay down His life for you and for me—for all of us.

Why is this so important?

Have you ever been dismissed by friends, discredited by a family member, or put down by a teacher or coach? Perhaps you have been betrayed by loved ones or by your best friend in the world. If you are breathing, I am almost certain that you have been rejected, abandoned, slandered, lied about, criticized, and bombarded with so many negative statements that in certain areas you don't think much of yourself. Some of us survive the shark tank of life and thrive anyway, but all of us tend to carry scars and memories that hold us back from embracing our true purpose.

Certain people are proud and arrogant—they think more highly of themselves than they should, and God cannot bless those heart conditions. However, most of us—including many of the proud ones—secretly or openly look at our own lives and think we are worthless or destined to fail in some way. We often hide these thoughts behind an extreme work ethic or a wall of false pride and bravado. In some cases we've allowed destructive words from others to sink in so deeply that we believe we are just trash. We accept the false claim that there is nothing good in our lives, even after we have received Jesus as Lord of our lives!

> God doesn't measure value the way the world measures. His divine measure begins and ends with the fact that He loves you.

People who don't value themselves generally don't value other people properly either. This is your day to be awakened to God's goodness, graciousness, and mercy. He loves you and values you for who you are.

Jesus loves people not because they are powerful, have money, or are beautiful or handsome. He simply loves them. In fact, He looks at you and me, and He sees what He made us to be. He made us for His purpose and His glory. Scripture says God loved us so much that

> even when we were dead in trespasses, made us alive together with Christ (by grace you have been saved), and raised us up together, and made us sit together in the heavenly places in Christ Jesus. (Ephesians 2:5–6)

That means you are royalty if you've accepted Jesus Christ as Lord! He has made you a king and a priest, and because of His supreme act of self-sacrifice, you have been accepted into the family of God (see Ephesians 1:6 and Revelation 5:10)! Let me repeat: you were not rejected; you are accepted!

The Bible says that if you are "in Christ," then you have become "a new creation; old things have passed away; behold, all things have become new" (2 Corinthians 5:17).

We are talking about the value God places on your life. He doesn't measure value the way the world measures. His divine measure begins and ends with the fact that He loves you. That love originated with God, and it stands beyond the reach or influence of any person's opinion, judgment, criticism, or rejection! This is your day to rise up and to accept and declare this truth: "God values my life. He counts me as someone important to Him."

You are special.

You have a purpose on this planet.

You have a job to complete.

God will use you for something that is great, but do first things first. Today, rise up and accept the fact that God loves you unconditionally.

"God, You Made My Life Miserable!"

JAMIE'S STORY

I was born into a very dysfunctional home filled with alcohol and abuse. *Darkness* is the only word that describes it.

Years have passed, yet I still vividly remember my dad drinking and beating my mother. She would leave and stay away for a couple of days, and we were always afraid to stay with my father. We just learned to not talk about our feelings.

By age four, I had already developed symptoms of an eating disorder due to the stress. I acted out, exhibited hyperactivity, and couldn't control my emotions in a balanced way, so I began seeing a psychiatrist when I was five.

Three years later, Mom went to work, and we went to a child-care facility where I was sexually abused. Another man in our hometown was sexually abusing me as well at the time.

By age twelve, I started coping with the abuse by drinking hard liquor, smoking marijuana and cigarettes, and by stealing compulsively for the thrill.

At the same time, I despised myself so much that I wanted to punish myself. I thought I deserved to have physical pain, so I cut myself with knives.

Despite my emotional pain over the abuse and abandonment, I couldn't cry. When I felt as if I wanted to cry, I'd cut instead. In those years, I always referred to the blood as "my tears."

You might be shocked to know that I was popular at school. I was a cheerleader, a dancer, and a gymnast—but I felt completely dead inside.

I hated being at home because they didn't want me there. No one was happy being there.

When I was eighteen, I ran away as soon as I graduated in order to embark on a new journey, one that became a living hell. My weight dropped drastically because I couldn't eat—I went from one hundred thirty pounds down to eighty-five pounds!

During that time I was diagnosed with borderline personality disorder, bipolar disorder, general anxiety disorder, major depressive disorder, attention deficit disorder, posttraumatic stress disorder, anorexia, bulimia, insomnia, and still another disorder whose name I always forget. I was being medicated for all of those things at the same time.

Two documented nervous breakdowns and several attempted suicides followed. I used to make myself throw up, and I wouldn't sleep for a week at a time.

With all of the addictions, I worked four jobs just to pay for it all. I would take a lot of pills so that I could face people at work. I didn't want to be around anybody. Finally, an oral infection due to bulimia took me within three days of death.

I just cried out to God, *You made my life miserable! Obviously You want me to die miserably to teach families to love their children.*

I did everything that I could to kill myself that week. In desperation, I searched on the Internet for ways to commit suicide, and Mercy Ministries of America popped up on the screen—a treatment center for girls. I broke down and just started crying. That was when my life began to change.

Hope seemed to rise in my heart that night. I entered Mercy as a resident, and I still remember sitting on my bed that first night. I cried and cried for the first time in a long time. I remember telling God, *This isn't it, this isn't it. I'm so sorry. Please forgive me.*

Later I went back to my hometown for the first time in years, and I learned within two weeks that I just wasn't ready for it. Slowly my life fell victim once again to wrong choices and negative thoughts. I began to think about how bad and ugly I was, and how rejection had virtually destroyed my life.

I was consumed with the thought, *I'm fat and I am so hated.*

The problem is that these things were no longer the truth because Jesus Christ had made me a new creation. Sadly, I was living in my old self, and I refused to believe God's Word.

One day I broke apart a razor and used the four blades to carve the word *fat* in my upper arm. Then I carved the word *hated* in my lower arm. Why? That was all that came to my mind—I was consumed with the thought, *I'm fat and I am so hated.* Then I took a handful of pills and landed in critical care.

My thoughts were desperate as I pleaded with God to let me die: *God, why am I here? Can You please just let me die? I have tried this so many times—I just want to leave this place. There's nothing good left for me. And I'm hurting every day. Just let me leave this world.*

The Lord was so gentle that His love changed my life. He told me, *Jamie, you don't know the plans I have for you...and this isn't part of My plan for you. I do have plans for you, but you keep trying to do your own. I'm going to keep intervening.*

His love broke through because He is my Father. I honestly feel like I'm His daughter and that I have the attributes that He has. I'm never going to be perfect, but I can strive for excellence. I will be the best person and the best imitator of Christ that I can be.

The only reason I've been kept alive and the only reason why I chose to live is Jesus. He is my passion and my calling. He is what I live for.

I know that He can use my life to help others and to be an encouragement because no one's life is a waste! And what about those things Satan intends for your harm? God turns them into good. I know that God loves me unconditionally. There is nothing—nothing—that can separate me from God's love.

○ ○ ○ ○ ○

YOUR VALUE DOESN'T FLUCTUATE—BECAUSE GOD'S LOVE IS CONSTANT

Think about it! You are valuable because of the price that was paid for you. What was that price? The highest price ever paid. What's it worth?

Have people told you, "You are worthless. You're of no account. There's no reason you should be on the planet"? I have got a better message—a true message for you:

God gave His Son for you. Jesus willingly gave His blood for you and paid the ultimate price to give you the ultimate gift—eternal life with Him!

If you haven't ever looked at yourself this way, I understand. The shallow culture of the world seems to judge all of us by our physical appearance. Just as soon as you get skinny enough, then you find the trend has changed—suddenly you aren't curvy enough. You no sooner pay a fortune for the latest fashion in basketball shoes than you discover no one who is anyone wears basketball shoes anymore.

Perhaps you've gone through life enduring scorn and rejection because of a physical impairment or a speech impediment. You may be absolutely beautiful on the outside but feel ugly and dirty on the inside because of something terrible that happened earlier in your life.

Listen my friend, true beauty does not come from the outside; it comes from what is on the inside. God looks at us in very special ways, but one truth always remains: God sees you very differently from the way the world does.

Jesus reached down to those whom the world rejected, and He valued them all the same. No matter how the world has categorized you and tried to put you in a box, today is the day to get out of that box. Leap out of that judgment trap and stop judging yourself according to the shifting, self-destructive standards of the world.

Perhaps you have heard the story of a young girl who was violated by her father. She was also told over and over again that she was worthless. Rejected, abused, and victimized, this girl could have lived as a victim the rest of her life, but she discovered her value in God! Today, all around the world, people are familiar with the name of this remarkable woman… Joyce Meyer. Through her messages, television broadcasts, and books, she has helped millions of people discover their value in God's eyes.

Sometimes folks look at people like Joyce—people who are in prominent positions of influence—and say, "Oh, you must have had it great growing up! Look, you had all of these wonderful things." No, Joyce Meyer's life was a nightmare…but that all changed because of the grace of our loving God.

Your life can be changed in just the same way!

God's grace can lift you no matter what has happened to you in the past. He says you are valuable no matter how often people have treated you as though you are unwanted, unwelcome, and unworthy! Joyce often heard herself referred to as trash, but she refused to accept someone else's label. She had already heard what God had to say about her, and that was all she needed!

Now you can make the same decision: will you listen to man or listen to God? Just declare it out loud: "I will not accept someone else's label of my life when it contradicts what God has said about me!"

You are valuable because of the price that was paid for you and the purpose God has for you. God created you and then saved you for the purpose of touching someone else's life! When you give your love away, it brings healing, deliverance, and the light of love to someone else. And that is what it means to be like Jesus.

God is counting on you. He knows who you are and where you live. He even knows the number of hairs on your head (and how many you've lost). He knows everything about you—and He still loves you!

WHAT DOES GOD THINK AND SAY ABOUT YOU?

- "Before I formed you in the womb I knew you" (Jeremiah 1:5).
- "For I know the thoughts that I think toward you, says the LORD, thoughts of peace and not of evil, to give you a future and a hope" (Jeremiah 29:11).
- "Being confident of this very thing, that He who has begun a good work in you will complete it until the day of Jesus Christ" (Philippians 1:6).
- "For we are His workmanship, created in Christ Jesus for good works, which God prepared beforehand that we should walk in them" (Ephesians 2:10).
- "For He has clothed me with the garments of salvation, He has covered me with the robe of righteousness" (Isaiah 61:10).

- "I will praise You, for I am fearfully and wonderfully made; marvelous are Your works, and that my soul knows very well" (Psalm 139:14).
- "For I am persuaded that neither death nor life, nor angels nor principalities nor powers, nor things present nor things to come, nor height nor depth, nor any other created thing, shall be able to separate us from the love of God which is in Christ Jesus our Lord" (Romans 8:38–39).
- "Yet in all these things we are more than conquerors through Him who loved us" (Romans 8:37).
- "Surely goodness and mercy shall follow me all the days of my life; and I will dwell in the house of the LORD forever" (Psalm 23:6).

You were created to be a champion of God! You are valuable because your value is measured by the price paid to redeem you. Your price was the life of the One who purchased you, the Son of God who now owns you. If you've accepted Jesus Christ as your Lord and Savior, then the King of the universe owns your life. And He has made you His own off-spring; you are a child of the King! Literally, you are royalty, one who is fully accepted into God's family with all of the rights and privileges of belonging to the King's family.

Your life cost the death and the innocent blood of Jesus Christ. He chose to give His life because He thought you were worth it! His opin-ion outweighs all others. So take all of those painful memories of the times you felt trashed, put down, rejected, and degraded—include those dark times when you wrestled unsuccessfully with a spirit of depression or even contemplated suicide—and put them up against what God says about you. The King wins, and so do you!

Don't check out of this life—we need you. God has a plan and a pur-pose for you, and He has already proven that you are valuable to Him.

Your life has a purpose and a plan crafted especially for you by your lov-ing Creator. He has even assigned people to your life that you are uniquely equipped to reach for Christ and to touch in a special way.

The Lord has also given you great potential. You are valuable in countless ways, and it doesn't matter what other people have said or done in their ignorance. God cares, and He declares that you are valuable.

8

Rising Above Your Circumstances

Life has its **ups and downs**.

But no matter how **low** you go…
    sickness
    poverty
    pain
    abuse
    loneliness
    despair
    darkness

You **don't have to stay** there. Even when you're feeling…
    down and out
    out of a job
    out of the house
    out of strength
    out of love
    out of hope

Keep your chin up.

Look **up.**

That's **where Christ is**...where your life is...where your real life is.

He will be your...
  about-face
  resting place
  saving grace

He will **raise you up** above...
  your past
  your hurts
  your mistakes
  your addictions
  your family tree
  your glass ceiling

You can rise above.

What is your greatest **accomplishment**?

What is the greatest challenge you've faced?

They were big, yes, but God has even **greater things** in store for you.

You can rise above any circumstance you face today! Your problems and obstacles may not go away instantly, but they will lose any power they possess to blow you away with the feeling that you are helpless, hopeless, and at the end of your rope.

God is on your side! He promised to supply you with all the wisdom you need. He offers to give you the strength and ability to do what He has called you to do!

Think about Noah, the man God warned about the Flood that would destroy all flesh because of virtually universal wickedness and evil. He was told he would build an ark to escape the flood—and take his family and a complete set of land-bound animals with him. And in the end Noah and his family escaped that flood. How did it happen? First, Noah had to hear God, then he had to do something about what he had heard. God told Noah what to do, providing specific instructions on how to build the ark. As a result, when the whole world went into liquidation, Noah was floating on his assets.

God planned way ahead of time for Noah and his family to survive.

He has a way for you to survive too, no matter what happens in the world around you.

You can rise above devastation, destruction, and seemingly impossible circumstances, just as Noah did. The final word on your life hasn't been delivered simply because you've been given a negative diagnosis or because there are problems in your home! You can change the message and alter the story of your life by living in God's Word!

God spoke to man named Isaac who grew desperate after famine struck his region. First he moved into Philistine territory near modern-day Gaza in southern Israel. Then Isaac decided to go to Egypt's Nile River Delta where there was plenty of water and fertile land. That is when the Lord appeared to Isaac and said, "Don't go down to Egypt; stay where I tell you. Stay here in this land and I'll be with you and bless you. I'm giving you and your children all these lands, fulfilling the oath that I swore to your father Abraham" (Genesis 26:2–3, MSG).

God also spoke to Abraham in advance, promising that He would bless him and his descendants (this would include the as-yet-unborn Isaac) in the land where He called them to be—the land we know today as Israel. Abraham journeyed to Gerar the first time, also during a great drought. Later his son, Isaac, moved to and settled in the same region at God's command to receive the promise during a second drought.

Isaac and his large family moved to Gerar even though the ground was totally dry. After God said, "Stay here…," Isaac settled in for the long haul. He sowed his seed in the land by faith, despite the drought conditions around him. A modern translation of the Bible says:

> That year Isaac's crops were tremendous! He harvested a hundred times more grain than he planted, for the LORD blessed him.
> He became a rich man, and his wealth only continued to grow.
> (Genesis 26:12–13, NLT)

Isaac planted seeds in the middle of a searing drought, and it seems that rain fell on his crops without falling anywhere else! The Philistine farmers around him saw it all, watching their crops wither while Isaac's produced a hundredfold return, making him richer and richer!

> **Y**ou can rise above devastation, destruction, and seemingly impossible circumstances.

It comes as no surprise that according to the biblical account these people envied him (see Genesis 26:14)! Think about it: do people envy someone who is experiencing the same thing they are? No, it seems that during that drought something different was happening to Isaac, and it defied natural explanation! His blessings motivated their envy. (I've noticed that God's blessings and favor can even be embarrassing sometimes when His gifts make us seem too different.)

Count on it: God is able to make a difference in your life too! As one of God's kids, you don't have to deny that bad or unsettling things are happening all around you in the economy, in society, or in some government crisis. Just say, "I have a God who has laws that can override what is happening in the universe. Through His law of sowing and reaping, God brings us supernatural blessings as we give to Him."

In love and obedience we plant our tithes and offerings in the soil of His faithfulness, and He will bless us in the middle of a crisis when nearly everyone is suffering lack! God can cause rain to fall on your seed and produce an embarrassingly blessed harvest, even in the middle of a drought—in your finances, marriage, business, or emotions! He is not limited like you and I—He can provide for you supernaturally.

Take courage! Don't let the things you see or hear on the news dominate your heart. Don't let the confusing or discouraging thoughts that the Enemy brings darken your mind. The Bible tells us to take "every thought captive to the obedience of Christ" (2 Corinthians 10:5, NASB).

Don't be overwhelmed! Instead, let God's promises come alive inside of you. Rise above your circumstances!

"God Couldn't Ever Use a Person Like Me"

THE MINISTRY OF CARMEN GIL

My childhood is a sad story of survival without money or family. By the time I was seven or eight years old, I had learned to clean for other people so that they would give me something to eat.

I grew up with no one to look to and no role model to help me form my self-image or my dreams. I never had any plans for my life; I was just happy to finish the day. That was good enough for me. I really didn't have any hopes or dreams.

As an adult, I found myself at church one day, and somebody said, "You, lady, you." When I turned around I realized this person was talking to me. This person said, "God is speaking to me that you will preach the gospel."

I thought, *Oh, she's insulting God now. He couldn't ever use a person like me. She just doesn't know me—that's why she's saying all these things over me.* Then the thought came into my mind: *You couldn't keep a husband, you destroyed your first marriage; you couldn't finish school, and you also destroyed your second marriage. You've messed up everything in your life, and it's because you're not a good person. You are so stupid! You're good for nothing and your life has no value. Now your kids will grow up just like you.*

I've always fought these kinds of thoughts, but after that prophecy, my desire to fulfill the will of God grew. I began to spend every extra dollar I had on teaching tapes. I listened to Bible teaching eight hours at a time as I cleaned houses·and prayed in the Spirit. I fell in love with Jesus Christ and began to constantly experience His presence.

When it comes to the calling of God in our lives, we shouldn't focus on the things that we can do; it should be on what God can do through us.

When I started my ministry, I didn't have the full picture of what God had for me, but I acted on what I did know. I took little steps to teach and to preach.

We started with eight people and increased to one hundred as I began to fulfill God's plan for my life. All of a sudden we had a congregation of three hundred, and then five hundred.

Today, we have the largest Spanish-speaking congregation in Tulsa—with fifteen hundred members! So God has fulfilled the dream that He has given me to preach the gospel.

But not every day is perfect... One day I was discouraged after preaching a message that I didn't think had gone very well. Then a little boy tugged at my clothes and said, "Pastora, Pastora! What did you do to my mother?" I asked him, "Son, what do you mean by that?" He said, "Pastora, for the first time my mom told me that she loves me! And she held me and kissed me!"

It touched me so deeply that I prayed, *Lord Jesus, as long as I live, if I can preach the gospel on radio or television, in the street, on a horse, or while walking or running—I'll do it. I will preach wherever I am, because I know that Your love is so real that it can heal families. It can turn the heart of a mother to love her children, and it is the answer. It is exactly what people are looking for.*

I am in the place that I am because of the grace of God. I am a trophy of the mercy of God. He's big enough to conquer our fears and our depression. He is a Father to the fatherless. He is *our* Father—and He can make all our dreams come to pass.

○ ○ ○ ○ ○

NO MATTER WHAT PEOPLE SAY, GOD HAS A PLAN TO LIFT YOU UP!

God can lift you above every negative circumstance associated with your birth and childhood! He delights in transforming and elevating the world's so-called nobodies to places of power and authority. Mary sang these words after God chose her to bring God's Son into the world: "He has put down the mighty from their thrones, and exalted the lowly" (Luke 1:52).

He will do the same thing in your life. Look to Him. The power of faith can help you rise above your circumstances. Release the spirit of faith to believe God's Word. Now begin to speak it!

I encourage you to recognize the lies the devil has spoken about you…and to throw them out! If someone said something to trash you, disrespect you, or put you down, don't believe it. Believe what God says. He says that you are valuable, special, and important. God says that He has a purpose for you.

Gideon lived in the land of negative circumstances too. The Bible says his land was surrounded by hostile foreign powers who took away all their food and kept the Israelites impoverished (see Judges 6:1–6).

When God showed up, Gideon was hiding in a hole in the ground, an ancient winepress, trying to secretly harvest some grain out of sight from his enemies. "The Angel of the LORD appeared to him, and said to him, 'The LORD is with you, you mighty man of valor!'" (Judges 6:12).

And Gideon said, "Say what? Are you talking to me?" He certainly didn't see himself that way, but God saw him for what he could become. God wasn't interested in Gideon's circumstances. He spoke to Gideon about who he was—God's deliverer for His people (see Judges 6:14–16).

This man was neck-deep in horrible circumstances. He and his people were oppressed and beaten down, and everyone lived in poverty. As soon as they harvested something or started to make progress, these enemies would swoop in and steal everything. Gideon didn't see himself as the important one, and yet God chose him.

God looks past your temporary circumstances and problems. He sees you for who He has made you to be. You are a mighty warrior—God's child, destined for a life of valor!

FACE THE GIANT IN YOUR LIFE

Think about King David's wonderful story! When David's father sent him to the battlefield to deliver food to his older brothers, he found the Israelite army on one side of a valley and the Philistine army on the other side. In the middle stood a huge giant named Goliath, and no one wanted to fight him.

David watched that giant shout a challenge to the Israelite army, "Send someone to fight with me. If you win, then we'll be your slaves, but if I win, you will be our slaves." When everyone else shrank back, David said, "I'll go fight him!"

David was so confident because he realized this giant did not have a covenant with God. With faith in God's might, David ran to the battle shouting these words to Goliath:

You come to me with a sword, with a spear, and with a javelin.
But I come to you in the name of the LORD of hosts, the God of

the armies of Israel, whom you have defied. This day the LORD will deliver you into my hand. (1 Samuel 17:45–46)

The story of David and Goliath is told worldwide, and for a good reason! Is there a Goliath in your life boasting, "I'm going to enslave you, and you'll never be anything! Give it up because I'm going to rule your life!"?

You know what to do. Accept the fact that this battle won't be won through your strength, ability, or resources. Face your giant in the power of the mighty name of the Lord. God will raise you up. He will deliver that giant of poverty, lack, rejection, abandonment, fear, or divorce into your hands. Run to this battle with the Word of God in your heart and on your lips! God says you will rise above these circumstances. This is your day to rise up!

What Makes a Person Happy?

DONNA'S STORY

Don was a good person and he had a good heart, but he made a really bad decision that nearly destroyed his life, and mine too.

Both of us drank heavily, but my husband, Don, also started taking "crank" (a powerful but cheaper street form of crystal methamphetamine).

At first Don tried to control the drug, but the drug ended up controlling him. It left me feeling hopeless and trapped in a downward spiral with no way out. After dealing with it for a year, I took a whole bottle of pills one night, thinking I wouldn't wake up the next morning.

God preserved my life that night, and neither Don nor I wanted to go back to the world we came from. So we asked God to help us, to change us and our way of thinking. He did it! He even helped us find the church we attend today.

I remember sitting in church one day, feeling peace and love come over me. I didn't want to leave the service that day, because I just wanted to stay in that atmosphere of love and acceptance that I had never experienced before.

As my husband and I grew in the Lord, I realized I had to forgive my husband for what he had done, and I also had to forgive myself. A healing process took place inside of me when I started loving and serving children and other adults.

We learned to trust God with everything we were and all that we possessed. As we began to learn about giving, serving, and tithing, we began to step out in faith.

It was really difficult for me the first time Don tithed (gave 10 percent of his income). I thought about the people we owed, along with our bills and rent—and I had just learned that I was pregnant with our second child. So I asked, "Are you sure you want to do that?" Don said, "Yes, I have to do this." So he did—and we've been doing it ever since.

We wanted to have a company of our own, but we knew it was hard to build up a business while we also worked other jobs to put food on the table. It took time, endurance, and a lot of hard work, but we did it. We stuck with it and endured, sometimes working day and night. We just kept pushing and kept believing that God would get us to the other side.

Now we have five service vans and we're going strong. We know we have a successful business because we trusted God with everything. He fulfilled our every dream and did more than we could ever ask or imagine! I know this: if we had stayed in the atmosphere we used to live in, there's no way we would be where we are now.

○ ○ ○ ○ ○

You Were Born to Overcome

We have ministered throughout the years in different nations wracked by ethnic and religious violence, civil war, and other devastations. We have been to Cambodia, Rwanda, Sierra Leone, and Haiti. The Lord has told us to go where the need is the greatest at any given moment, where people are hurting. He's also told us to tell people that right in the middle of their worst problems, they can rise above them. In the face of the worst situations, we speak words of hope and love.

Listen. You may be thinking right now, *Man, you don't know what I'm going through. You don't know where I am or what's happening in my life.* I may not know everything about your situation, but God does. He cares about you. So do I…and I do know this about you:

- You were not born to grovel in the dust. You were born to overcome.
- You don't belong under Satan's feet, feeling tormented, oppressed, bound, rejected, and abandoned! You are meant to rise above it all.
- God has had a plan for you from the beginning, and He has a way to lift you up!

God's love is coming to you right now. He is saying, "I care about you. I value you. You are important to Me, and you can rise above this challenge!"

Lift your sights higher and see that there is a better way leading to a better day! Declare it by faith: "Life can change for me!"

When you lay hold of that, something miraculous will begin to happen as you put your trust in Jesus.

9

Second Chances

Have you **lost** your way?
> no compass
> no friends
> no hope

Have you been led **astray**?
> greener grass
> brighter lights
> bigger pastures

Lions, tigers, bears...

Oh, my!

Only to find there's no place like **home**...
> where the heart is
> where forgiveness is
> where your heavenly Father is

He will...
    heal your broken heart
    renew your troubled mind

His **promises** are true.

His mercies are new.

And He's **waiting** with open arms for you.

No matter where you've been or how far you've gone...

It's **never too late** to come home.

God is the God of the second chance, a God of mercy. In fact, the Bible says the Lord's mercies are new every morning (see Lamentations 3:22–23).

Did you fail yesterday? Perhaps you failed the day before. (Most of us have to ask ourselves, *Did I fail in the last hour?*) How can you start again?

There is only one way, and that is to look to God's mercy. He cares about you more than you could ever imagine!

After Jesus taught about forgiving others, Peter the disciple asked Jesus how many times he should forgive someone who had offended him. When Peter suggested seven times, Jesus said, "I do not say to you, up to seven times, but up to seventy times seven" (Matthew 18:22).

If the Lord tells us to forgive someone nearly five hundred times a day, then how much more will God forgive us? Do we really understand that it is God's mercy and grace that allow us to rise up from our failures, sins, and wrongdoing?

- His mercy withholds the punishment that you really deserve.
- God's grace gives you strength, blessings, provision, and favor that you could never earn or deserve.
- His mercy and grace work together on your behalf.

You probably know that even after you receive Jesus as Lord and Savior, you still sin (or miss the mark) from time to time. God's Word tells us what to do when that happens: "If we confess our sins, He is faithful and just to forgive us our sins and to cleanse us from all unrighteousness" (1 John 1:9).

> **R**emember, the Lord's tender mercies are new every morning.

You admit it and repent of it. It isn't enough to say "I'm sorry." You must turn your back on that thing and go the opposite direction—toward God's goodness. Then God faithfully forgives you, cleanses you of all unrighteousness, and removes those sins. Psalm 103:11–12 declares, "For as the heavens are high above the earth, so great is His mercy toward those who fear Him; as far as the east is from the west, so far has He removed our transgressions from us." In other words, those sins are long gone! God also said that He would "cast all our sins into the depths of the sea" and "remember [them] no more" (Micah 7:19 and Hebrews 10:17).

Perhaps the greatest things about God are His love, mercy, and grace. He cares for you more than you could ever imagine. He constantly knocks on the door of your heart, hoping that you will open up and receive His love and forgiveness.

If you struggle with the hidden suspicion that God is judging and condemning you because He hates you, I have some good news for you! Jesus said that He did not come to condemn the world but to save the world. He died for you even while you were still a sinner (see John 3:17 and Romans 5:8)! That is unconditional, sacrificial love. God loves you on your worst day and in your worst mess just as much as He loves you on your best day. It is that God kind of love that can pull you out of sin and give you victory in your life!

Now this is your day to live and walk in the mercy of God and depend on His forgiveness. Remember, the Lord's tender mercies are new every morning.

Breaking the Cycle That Made Me Homeless

PHIL'S STORY

I was looking for the love that only God can give us, but I was searching in all the wrong places. I discovered He can't be found in the bottom of a beer bottle, and He's not at the end of a blunt [marijuana cigar] or a joint.

I grew up in a Christian family with a great mother and father who were faithful to serve in the church. I remember surrendering my life to Jesus Christ in summer camp and carrying my Bible to school (in those days, it seemed to take a lot more boldness).

In my teen years I became involved in athletics, and that brought a whole new crowd into my life. I began to go with them to parties and started engaging in various unhealthy activities.

Later in college, I joined a fraternity and started drinking more. After I graduated from college, I got married and had a daughter. That life lasted about three years...then came the divorce.

I spent eleven years working in a good industry, bought a home, and enjoyed some stability, but all that time I was drinking. Then I started going to bars and got involved in pool leagues, where I devoted nearly all of my off-hours to playing pool and drinking heavily.

My employer asked me if I had a drinking problem, and I said, "No, no. I don't have any problem with drinking."

Yet, as I continued my heavy drinking habit, I collected a few DUIs and wound up going to prison. After I finally qualified for the work-release program, I started working for a fast-food place. I had to walk to work every day and return to lockup each night.

Finally, I made pre-parole and got my own apartment, but I had to walk three miles to and from work every day.

One morning I was walking to work and it was bitterly cold outside. I put out my thumb, hoping to catch a ride. After I watched car after car go by—and no one offered me a ride—I walked out into the middle of the street and began to shout less-than-flattering things at people. I'm not proud of it, but I was upset because no one seemed to have any concern for me. I was looking for a little compassion and hope.

People pass you by and look right through you, as if you weren't even there.

Despite my recent jail stay, I started drinking heavily again, and my alcoholism led to my being late to work a couple of times. When I called in late for a third time, the shift manager at the restaurant decided he no longer needed my services.

Without that job, I couldn't pay my rent. Since I had been more determined to keep my bar bill current than pay rent, I was already behind. That is the pathetic cycle of an alcoholic—the cycle that helped me become a homeless statistic.

People who have never been homeless have no idea what it is like to be homeless, to be looked down upon by other people. People pass you by and look right through you, as if you weren't even there.

I wound up sleeping under a bridge. I remember the night a rat bit my ear. I suspect I smelled so bad that the rat thought I was dead...

Homeless or not, I still had to report to my parole officer. Since I had a five-year suspended sentence from a previous case, I knew a nice set of silver bracelets was waiting for me when I went into the parole office...and there was.

The morning before I reported for prison, I drank a couple of beers because I knew that was going to be the last time I'd have the opportunity for quite sometime.

Later, in the bone-chilling cold of that holding cell, I reflected on my childhood—a time when I had been close to the Lord. The Holy Spirit began to work in my heart, and I almost felt like crying when I realized just how destitute I had become. That was when I realized I was definitely on the path to destruction. I so wanted to go back to those days when I was close to the Lord.

I spent a total of seventeen months in prison. During that time, my life was totally transformed. On November 28, 1996, I gave my life back to the Lord and decided never to go back to that lifestyle. And I never did—and never will.

I was like the prodigal son in Jesus' parable who went out and spent his father's wealth in a far country. When I finally came home, I discovered the heavenly Father was there waiting for me with open arms, full of love and compassion.

○ ○ ○ ○ ○

GET BACK IN THE GAME!

Do God's mercy and grace give believers the freedom to keep sinning? No, His mercy and grace provide the power to walk away from sin and live in freedom, to enjoy the benefits of righteous and holy lives. But sometimes people receive the Lord and then fall back into their ungodly habits or sinful lifestyles. They often feel they can never be forgiven again. If this has happened to you, I have good news: there is a second chance! Even if you have tried many times to break free from something and you just can't—don't give up! You may not be where you want to be, but the fact that you're reading this right now and paying attention should give you confidence that you are headed for a better day. God has a plan, a purpose, and the power to lift you up so that you can hit the mark He set for you.

Peter's story gives hope to those of us who feel we just can't get it right. He is one of the disciples who traveled with Jesus from the beginning of His ministry to the day He was crucified. A rugged fisherman from Galilee, Peter left his nets and boat to follow Jesus.

Very few men matched Peter's commitment to Jesus. He genuinely cared about the Lord and was the first human being to say, "You are the Christ, the Son of the living God" (Matthew 16:16). Jesus replied that only God the Father could have given this insight about who He really was (see Matthew 16:17). Peter was all out for Jesus. Whatever he thought he should do for or with Jesus, he went after it wholeheartedly (of course, sometimes he led with his mouth rather than with his heart). In fact when Jesus told His disciples that trouble was coming and that they were going to deny Him, Peter boldly said: "Even if all are made to stumble because of You, I will never be made to stumble" (Matthew 26:33).

Jesus immediately corrected Peter by saying that Peter would deny

Jesus three times that very night before a crowing rooster signaled day-break. Peter stubbornly claimed he wouldn't deny Jesus, even if he had to die with Him—and the rest of the disciples chimed in with him! (A leader going in the wrong direction tends to take people along with him!) Later that night, every prediction Jesus had made came true. He was arrested and taken to the High Priest's residence for questioning. It was there that Peter's courage failed. Some servant girls and other bystanders accused him of being a follower of Jesus, and Peter—as predicted—denied it. He even cursed for added emphasis the last two times he insisted "I do not know the Man!" (Matthew 26:72). Sure enough, after his third denial, Peter heard a rooster crow at daybreak and his heart broke.

Think about it: This man who denied Jesus had spent almost three and a half years at His side. Peter had participated in the miracles and played a key role in His ministry, but then Peter denied Jesus three times, cursed about it, and ran and hid! If anyone needed a second chance, it was Peter!

How did Jesus deal with this total failure in Peter's life? Did He go over every detail of his miserable performance? Did the Lord remind Peter of how he had let Him down? Did He rehearse the way Peter had cursed while publicly denying Him? No, the Bible says Jesus simply asked Peter three times if he loved Him, and in reply to Peter's affirmation, Jesus told him each time—"Feed and tend My sheep" (see John 21:15–17).

On the day of Pentecost, fifty days after Jesus was crucified, God poured out His Spirit on the believers who were gathered together. And who did God choose to preach the first sermon in church history? Peter! And three thousand people gave their life to Christ in response to Peter's message (see Acts 2).

Do you or someone you care about feel as if life has hit bottom? The world may have rejected and abandoned you, and all you can think about are the verbal missiles launched toward you: "You are worthless. After what you've done, you can never get back!" Just remember how Jesus picked up Peter after his failures. God is saying to you—and to all of us who feel discouraged or disqualified—"Get back in the race, and go love the people I've called you to love."

DO YOU REALLY THINK GOD GIVES SECOND CHANCES?

There was a man who had two sons. The younger one said to his father, "Father, give me my share of the estate." So he divided his property between them.

Not long after that, the younger son got together all he had, set off for a distant country and there squandered his wealth in wild living. After he had spent everything, there was a severe famine in that whole country, and he began to be in need. So he went and hired himself out to a citizen of that country, who sent him to his fields to feed pigs. He longed to fill his stomach with the pods that the pigs were eating, but no one gave him anything.

When he came to his senses, he said, "How many of my father's hired men have food to spare, and here I am starving to death! I will set out and go back to my father and say to him: Father, I have sinned against heaven and against you. I am no longer worthy to be called your son; make me like one of your hired men." So he got up and went to his father.

But while he was still a long way off, his father saw him and was filled with compassion for him; he ran to his son, threw his arms around him and kissed him.

The son said to him, "Father, I have sinned against heaven and against you. I am no longer worthy to be called your son."

But the father said to his servants, "Quick! Bring the best robe and put it on him. Put a ring on his finger and sandals on his feet. Bring the fattened calf and kill it. Let's have a feast and celebrate. For this son of mine was dead and is alive again; he was lost and is found." So they began to celebrate. (Luke 15:11–24, NIV)

The prodigal son's father was watching and waiting for his son to come home. Jesus wants us to understand that our heavenly Father is watching and waiting for you and me as well! When we fall into sin or wander due to our pain, He is waiting for us to come home. He is ready to come running to greet you and me!

Most of us hear that story and visualize ourselves running toward God, but in the picture Jesus described in this parable, the father was running to embrace his long-lost son. Our Father is waiting to run to receive and embrace you too. He is patiently waiting to receive you, welcome you home, to tell you how much He loves you!

Our heavenly Father wants us to know that His plans for us are still for good and not evil. The power of the blood of Jesus has wiped away every evil or wrongful thing that has taken place in our lives. He wants us to know that those things have not disqualified us from being His sons and daughters.

Jesus is speaking directly to you and those you care about, offering forgiveness and mercy. Your Father in heaven is ready to run to you and to restore your dignity as a member of His family! The Bible says you are "accepted in the Beloved" (Ephesians 1:6), and God's wonderful plan for you is still the same—to bring you love, mercy, forgiveness, and a future!

The prodigal son stepped right back into his special relationship with his father; he wasn't punished with a demotion from son to hired hand. Have you been reluctant to turn back to God because you've felt that you were unworthy? The truth is that no one is worthy on his or her own merits. Don't think that your sin is really big, while the sins other people commit really aren't much. God says all sin is evil, and all sin separates us from Him. Jesus paid for that sin with His blood and canceled it out. This is the foundation of our second chance in God's love!

Still having doubts about whether God can redeem your life, your situation? Consider this next story. One day some men brought a woman to Jesus who had been caught in the act of adultery (there is no mention of why they didn't bring in the guilty man as well). They threw her at Jesus' feet and cited the law that stipulated she should be stoned on the spot. Jesus seemed to ignore their words. He simply stooped near the ground and began to write in the sand, while the men holding stones demanded judgment without mercy. Finally, Jesus said, "He who is without sin among you, let him throw a stone at her first" (John 8:7). Then He started writing in the dirt again. Something about what Jesus wrote in the sand—perhaps a list of the sins each man had committed—made every one of them drop the stones and slink away, from the oldest to the youngest. Jesus looked at the woman after everyone had left and said:

> "Woman, where are those accusers of yours? Has no one condemned you?"
> She said, "No one, Lord."
> And Jesus said to her, "Neither do I condemn you; go and sin no more." (John 8:10–11)

This is the power of forgiveness, and it is why anyone who fails miserably gets a second chance from God! If you feel like you've sinned or failed so badly that you can never be forgiven or start over, Jesus Christ is saying these words right now to you:

I am giving you the power to rise above everything that has happened in the past! Confess your sins and failures; turn away from them and give them to Me. Now say out loud, "Lord, I receive Your mercy."

This is your time to rise up and do what God has called you to do! He has assigned you a very important purpose on this earth. In other words, your life counts!

Someone else desperately needs what you have received. God didn't give you a second chance just to help you—He also meant for you to bring that love and forgiveness out into the world. Now be faithful and share with others the good news of God's gift of a second chance.

10

Restoration

Has your life been **trashed**?
    broken?
    crushed?
    shattered?
    wrecked?
    …beyond repair?

Do you feel destined for the **junkyard**? It's a good thing God **recycles**.

He turns…
    trash into treasure
    rags into riches
    paupers into princes

You might be down in the dumps, but **God is not afraid** to dig through your garbage.
    When we see holes…
    He sees wholeness.

When we see rubbish…
He sees righteousness.
When we see death…
He sees life.

He **makes**…
beauty out of ashes
joy out of sorrow

He can…
redeem your past
rebuild your future

So **before** you…
trash it
can it
dump it

Hand it over to **Jesus.**

Your life can be **restored.**

God is *the* master of restoration. He sent His only Son, Jesus, to heal the brokenhearted, bring good news to the poor, and to set people free from every kind of bondage and oppression!

Jesus launched His adult ministry and began His march to the cross with a shocking opening message in His hometown of Nazareth. Jesus was in the synagogue on the Sabbath when He took the scroll of Isaiah and stood up to read to the gathering of people: "The Spirit of the LORD is upon Me, because He has anointed Me to preach the gospel to the poor; He has sent Me to heal the brokenhearted, to proclaim liberty to the captives and recovery of sight to the blind, to set at liberty those who are oppressed; to proclaim the acceptable year of the LORD" (Luke 4:18–19, quoting Isaiah 61:1–2).

After Jesus closed the scroll of Isaiah, gave it to the attendant, and sat down, He announced to everyone in the synagogue, "You've just heard Scripture make history. It came true just now in this place" (Luke 4:20, MSG).

The people were shocked because Jesus dared to declare that He was the fulfillment of this passage they had heard and studied throughout their lives. He was saying that He is the Healer, the Restorer, and the Deliverer. He is literally the Jubilee—the Old Testament season when land, freedom, and position were restored to every descendant of Abraham, even if they had somehow landed in slavery or poverty.

The Year of Jubilee is a picture of the year of God's favor. Now we, too, can walk in God's favor every day of our lives, because all of God's blessings to us are wrapped up in one package—Jesus! He was and is every good thing the Old Testament had pointed to and everything the New Testament promises!

The Bible is like no other book in human history. Think of it: God's Book was written over a period of fifteen hundred years by forty different authors in a total of sixty-six different books! Yet His Word has one theme woven together in perfect harmony, pointing to God's love for humankind and the coming of the Savior, Jesus Christ.

Why were the people shocked when Jesus announced that the promise of God's goodness had come to pass? Because only the "Real Thing" could make that claim! When sin entered the earth, it brought brokenness, destroyed lives, torn families, hatred, bitterness, rejection, abandonment, divorce, and death. And that meant we would lose our treasured relationships, loved ones, and possessions.

Are you experiencing some type of loss in your life? Has a great pain gripped your life, causing you to feel as if there is no way out? Perhaps you feel beaten down by your sense of loss—and the pain that loss brings. This is God's message for you today: Jesus will heal your broken heart and restore what has been lost.

From that moment when Jesus spoke in the synagogue until today, the year of God's favor has continued because of what Jesus did for us on the cross. This is our time to receive all the benefits of God's restoration, abundance, and mercy.

A friend in Quito, Ecuador, told me about a man who came to a special prayer meeting and began to open his heart about his traumatic childhood. When he was three years old, his alcoholic father came in and began to beat him. He managed to escape his father's grasp and run out the door. He fled to the street and crawled under a car, where he lay awake all night until the next morning. When some dogs began to sniff around the car, and after his father had left for work, the boy crawled out and in terror ran back home.

What happened to that little boy? Somehow over the years, he met and surrendered his life to Jesus Christ and found healing in his heart. He forgave his father and was able to leave his past behind him. Now he is going on with what God has in store for his life.

You may have your own story of pain, agony, abuse, or violation at the hands of other people. God promises us in Joel 2:25, "I will restore to you the years that the swarming locust has eaten, the crawling locust, the consuming locust, and the chewing locust." Each of these four types of insect may have specialized in devouring different parts of a plant: one consumed the leaves, another the flower, and the remaining two might have consumed the stem and the branch. We do know that when they were done, nothing was left.

God is saying to you: "Although your whole life has been devastated, I will restore you." He said, "I will give you beauty for ashes, the oil of joy for mourning, the garment of praise for the spirit of heaviness" (see Isaiah 61:3).

More people than ever seem to be hurting. Are you one of them? Is your life marked by heaviness, depression, and fear over an uncertain future? remorse over an all-too-real past? suicidal thoughts? Let your faith rise as you read these words. Believe that God will do for you what He has done for countless others. His healing power cannot be stopped by those around you, as long as you believe. Rise up! This is your day to be made whole.

Is It Possible to Fix
a Broken Person?

THE KAMI DRAPER STORY

I had to grow up so fast that I couldn't be a kid. My parents lived for fast thrills, and it left the family broken and lost. They seemed to do everything possible to ruin their lives quickly, and in the process I was robbed of my childhood.

Dad was a sex addict and an abusive alcoholic. I was so afraid of him that at the young age of eleven, I started to keep a knife under my pillow for protection. When Dad was drunk, he often beat my mom. One day I told her that she was a fool for living there. "You need to get out," I said. She followed my advice and left—and she left me behind as well.

Dad responded by treating me like the woman of the house. I had to wash his clothes, make his bed, and keep the house spotless.

Before I even had a driver's license, Dad had me drive around town to pay the bills and buy groceries. It wasn't right, but I did it because I feared he might beat me like he did my mom.

One time he stood up and threw the kitchen table across the room, barely missing me. Then Dad started choking me as I sat in a kitchen chair. The chair fell backward onto the floor, and I was pinned there on my back, helpless to do anything but stare at him.

Dad's friend had to come and get him off me. The whole time he was saying, "Robert, just get off her! Get off her; leave her alone!"

I remember getting up and running to my room, where I just cried and cried.

Later that night after Dad went to bed, I called my mom. At that time she literally was living in a barn because she didn't have anywhere else to go. She broke and trained horses for a living, so she just lived there with the horses.

Mom said, "Well, pack your stuff, and we'll come get you when your dad's gone to work."

I lived with Mom in that barn—in a small feed room—for about a year. It was just a little square enclosure with a microwave and two lawn chairs that did double duty as our beds. That stay in the barn was the happiest time of my childhood. We didn't have anything, but at least I felt loved and safe.

Then one day Mom told me that she was going to go live with a man and that I had to go live back with my dad. I couldn't believe that she was leaving me again. This time it hurt even more, because she chose to love a stranger more than her own flesh and blood.

While all this was going on, a church started sending a bus to our neighborhood, inviting us to worship and offering us free pizza. Naturally, I started going for the food and fun. I soon discovered that these Christians were different; they weren't like any Christians I had ever seen before. They were actually the real deal. I wanted to be like them. They gave me a grip on hope. I thought, *If I can just grasp what they have, maybe my future with my family will turn out right.*

It depressed me to think that everyone I loved was going straight to hell—including my mom, my dad, and my siblings. I remember crying out in a bathroom one day, "Lord, please send somebody to help them! Send somebody to tell them how good You are and how real You are."

That was the first time I remember hearing God's voice clearly. He said, *I am sending you—I am sending you to tell them about Me. I am calling you into the ministry.* Right there I got on my knees and started praising God. "Lord, if You want me to go into the ministry, I will. I don't know anything about it, but I'm going to do it."

I wanted to see my family saved and their lives changed. All they had to do was see His love. I knew if they caught just a glimpse of it, then they would be hungry for it.

I went back to see my family and showed them the love of God in me. They wanted what I had! They saw God living in my life, and they wanted it in their own lives. They were hungry for the real thing.

Today, my dad is not the same man that he was back then. He has surrendered his life to Jesus and has been totally changed and transformed. I used to sleep with a knife under my pillow, waiting to kill him, but now I love Dad and I don't know what I would do without him in my life.

Do not lose hope! God restored everything that the Enemy stole from me. He gave me everything that I thought I could never have. He has made my life better than I ever imagined or dreamed!

God is bigger than all of your problems. Remember that He holds this world in His hands and can do anything. Nothing is impossible with God!

EMBRACE GOD'S PLAN FOR TRANSFORMING YOUR LIFE

When Jesus restores a life, He makes all things new! That is His promise for you too. Here are four powerful ways God transforms and restores you from the inside out!

First: God forgives your sins through the blood of Jesus. Sin can cause terrible devastation in your life. If you have experienced such devastation, then confess your sins and turn away from them. The Bible promises in 1 John 1:9 that God will be faithful and just to forgive you and to cleanse you of all unrighteousness.

Second: The power of the Holy Spirit helps you to forgive others. This is as important for you as it is for them. Perhaps some of the things you endured were so awful and terrible that you feel you just can't let them go. You may be right—you may not be able to forgive certain people in your own power. However, through the power of the Holy Spirit, you can speak words and mean them: "Father, I forgive [the person's name]."

Remember that sin comes out by confession. That is true for your own sin and for the sins of others as you forgive them. Declare out loud, "I forgive you." Even if they're not present or are now deceased, say: "Father, I forgive [the person's name] who did this to me." (Sometimes we must forgive a company, group, or organization—not just individuals.)

Third: Let the Word of God get inside of you. For instance, focus on the prophetic word in Joel 2:25, in which God promised His people He would restore everything that had been lost through devastating circumstances. Memorize and apply the promises Jesus declared in Luke 4:18–19:

The Spirit of the LORD is upon Me, because He has anointed
Me to preach the gospel to the poor; He has sent Me to heal the
brokenhearted, to proclaim liberty to the captives and recovery
of sight to the blind, to set at liberty those who are oppressed;
to proclaim the acceptable year of the LORD.

Put these scriptures in your heart and mind, and speak them with your mouth. You are literally transformed by renewing your mind with

God's Word! Whenever those old thoughts, feelings, or attitudes come back, move to the strategy in point four.

Fourth: Speak the name of Jesus and say "No!" to those thoughts, feelings, or attitudes. Declare with your mouth, "In the name of Jesus, I command every wrong thought, feeling, and attitude [name them specifically when possible] to leave my mind and heart!"

Remember that the name of Jesus is above every name! When you take your stand and claim the power of the blood of Jesus, the Holy Spirit, and the Word of God through the name of Jesus, then you release the awesome power of God into your situation! This will bring you true freedom every day of your life!

Recently I met a young lady who experienced a horrible rejection in her life. When her mother and father divorced, her father told her, "I don't want to have anything to do with you anymore." He had decided to start a new life with another woman and another family.

That young woman came to Oral Roberts University feeling broken and hurting. As she began to hear about the goodness of God and the grace and mercy available through the Lord Jesus, she let God work inside of her. Forgiveness and pardon began to flow through her heart and emotions, and she began to get healed.

She decided to write a letter to her father, hoping to reestablish a connection with him. She described what she was doing and how her life was going. She also explained why she was able to forgive and let go. The day finally came when a package arrived. She opened it to find all of her letters unopened, along with a message: "I told you: I don't want anything to do with you."

We can only imagine the pain of rejection the daughter felt—again— but she chose to forgive and go on—again. With God's grace and mercy, we can do all things.

She was one of the top graduates in her class of 2008, and the amazing thing about her story is that this young lady delivered a commencement address! I heard her share her story and thought it was one of the most powerful messages I'd ever heard. I thought, *How could it be? How could she forgive…again?* But I already knew the answer: it was the grace of God.

The Lord has a way of restoring our life despite the bad things that have happened. The Bible tells of Joseph and how he experienced this restoration power. As a young man, he was sold by his brothers into slavery due to violent sibling jealousy. Later, he was falsely accused of attempted rape by the wife of Pharaoh's chief jailer, Potiphar, and put in prison. And after he helped Pharaoh's butler in prison, the man forgot all about Joseph once he received his own freedom.

Think about it. How would you feel if members of your own family sold you into slavery in another country? And then you get slandered for doing the right thing, only to be thrown into an Egyptian dungeon and then forgotten by somebody you helped? Yet despite all of these bad experiences, Joseph held on.

During a crisis, the butler finally remembered Joseph and told Pharaoh about his friend who could interpret spiritual dreams. Pharaoh had him hauled out of the dungeon and shared his dreams with him. After Joseph successfully interpreted Pharaoh's dream, Egypt's ruler put him in charge of gathering grain for seven good years and then distributing it over seven bad years.

During those years of drought Joseph's brothers showed up, hoping to buy grain. They didn't recognize Joseph until he said, "I'm your brother" (see Genesis 45:3). They were terrified, assuming he would seek revenge for their betrayal years earlier. Instead, Joseph said, "You meant evil against me; but God meant it for good, in order to bring it about as it is this day, to save many people alive" (Genesis 50:20). Joseph was able to see beyond the evil things of his past and declare God's plan and purpose for his life—and for the lives of his loved ones!

> I pray that God will help you forget the
> pain of your past and receive
> His blessings and fruitfulness today!

Joseph's restoration is memorialized in the names of his two sons: Manasseh, which means "For God has made me forget all my toil and all my father's house" (Genesis 41:51), and Ephraim, which means "For God has caused me to be fruitful in the land of my affliction" (Genesis 41:52).

That is my prayer for you! I pray that God will help you forget the pain of your past and receive His blessings and fruitfulness today and in the future. He is the God who restores, and you are one of the children He loves.

Remember what He said in Jeremiah 29:11: "I know the plans that I have for you...plans for welfare and not for calamity to give you a future and a hope" (NASB). When the Lord said these words to Israel, things weren't looking good. Your life may not look so good now, but remember God's promise: "I have good plans for you." God is in the process of restoring you. His love, mercy, and grace are coming into your life.

It's time for you to believe God. David declared in Psalm 27:13, "I would have lost heart, unless I had believed that I would see the goodness of the LORD in the land of the living." I want you to believe that you will see God's goodness in the land of the living. He is walking you right out of that rejection, pain, and suffering! The power of Jesus Christ can set you free and keep you free.

The Rejected Boy
Who Reaches Thousands

BILL'S STORY

A man who experienced a horrible rejection as a little boy still remembers the day his mother dropped him off at a curb in an unfamiliar neighborhood and said, "Sit here, son. I'll be back for you." The last words he heard her say were, "I don't think I can handle it anymore."

She drove away, and he sat on that curb all afternoon. He stayed there through the night and all the next day. He sat at that curb alone until the third day, waiting for his mother to return.

A man who noticed the boy on the curb came to a shocking realization: *This boy has been abandoned.* He tried unsuccessfully to help the boy reconnect with his mother and finally decided to take the boy into his own home.

The boy was raised by that family, and it was there that young Bill accepted Jesus Christ as his Lord and Savior. He went on to be trained in ministry.

Today, we know that little boy who was rejected as...Bill Wilson, the man who has the largest Sunday school in the whole world! Thanks to Bill, thousands of children are being reached in New York City and in other major cities around the world!

After years of tireless inner-city ministry, Bill says, "I still drive the bus [for our ministry], because every time I look into the eyes of one of those children and see their hurt and pain, I remember what I went through."

○ ○ ○ ○ ○

Your Time for Miracles

What ministry is going to come out of your pain and agony in life? How many people will be helped because God helped you? How many people who are suffering and bound will find hope because you are there to say, "You can rise up with Jesus' help!"?

You may be right in the middle of your suffering, rejection, and pain, but I am telling you right now that God has a purpose for your life. Let His life flow through you to others! He will do more than merely get you out of your mess. He will also help you to help others!

Allow the pain of your past to become a steppingstone to a higher life in Jesus. Let the light you have received become a star that shines through the darkness of others because of the power of Jesus Christ. Declare this out loud: "Lord Jesus, I receive Your healing for my broken heart. I receive Your restoration in my life. I receive Your help and strength so that I can help others find restoration."

This is your time for miracles!

11

Giving Thanks

Is your **glass**…
   half empty?
   half full?

What you see is what you get.

Feeling like your life is **on the rocks**?

Then take a moment to **remember** all that God
has given you…
   sun and moon
   hopes and dreams
   laughter
   song
   love
   forgiveness
   purpose

grace
new life
His only Son

So raise your glass to the One who fills it up. And say…

"Thank You!"

Now isn't that **refreshing**?

We have every reason to give thanks. Psalm 100:4–5 says:

Enter into His gates with thanksgiving,
    And into His courts with praise.
    Be thankful to Him, and bless His name.
For the LORD is good;
    His mercy is everlasting,
    And His truth endures to all generations.

Sometimes people say, "How can I give thanks? Do you really understand how bad my life is right now? And what about our economy? And how can I sleep at night, given all the terrible things that are happening on the other side of the world!"

Regardless of your circumstances, and they may be very difficult, my response doesn't change: God is good. His mercy is everlasting. His truth endures.

You can stand upon God's Word, and He will honor it in your life. His mercy toward you is not going to change. If you need forgiveness and pardon, you can receive it.

And if you're wondering why all the bad things happen, remember, they are not God's doing. God is a good God. Don't believe everything you see and hear on talk shows, on the Internet, in movies, or even in your insurance papers! (It seems that most insurance policies refer to natural catastrophes such as floods, hurricanes, volcano eruptions, earthquakes, and tornadoes as "acts of God.")

God is not the source of evil, accidents, or disease. Jesus said: "The thief [that's the devil] does not come except to steal, and to kill, and to destroy. I have come that they may have life, and that they may have it more abundantly. I am the good shepherd. The good shepherd gives His life for the sheep" (John 10:10–11).

God's will for you is good, not evil. He hasn't planned calamity or tragedy for you. Remember that the bad things that happen in this world are not the will of God for you. He created a perfect world. Evil came into the picture with the fall of Satan, who was once an archangel of God called Lucifer. When he rebelled and was instantly thrown down, a third of the angels followed him.

Adam and Eve joined that group unwittingly when they chose to disobey God at the urging of Satan, who appeared in the form of a serpent. Their action opened the door for sin, sickness, disease, and death to infect the entire human race. The evil and negative things that happen on this planet are not the will of God. They are the consequences of sin and rebellion.

Do you want to know what God's will is for you? Look at Jesus and how He treated people like you and me. He healed the sick, opened blind eyes, and delivered people in bondage from demons. He calmed the storm and multiplied loaves and fish to feed thousands. Can you see God's healing, delivering, and restoring response to the evil and harmful things of the world?

Today is a day to rejoice and celebrate, because we serve a good God whose mercy endures forever!

Many years ago Sharon and I worked at a retreat center in Minnesota. I led worship and Sharon played the piano in the evening meetings. During the day we worked in almost every area of the camp.

One day I became ill. My head was spinning and stuffed up. We were scheduled to wash dishes in the dining area right up to the time of the evening meeting. We finished our kitchen duties thirty minutes before the meeting, and I had no idea how I was going to lead worship that night on stage. I could barely open my mouth, let alone sing.

> **G**od is not the source of evil, accidents, or disease.

I went back to the tiny cabin where we were staying and laid down. Then the Lord said, *Get up and praise Me. Get up and give thanks.* Honestly, that was not what I wanted to hear. I didn't feel like doing anything but staying in bed, but I got up and began to say, "God, I just thank You that You are the Healer, You are the Deliverer! I thank You for Your mercy. I thank You for good health."

When I first began to praise and thank the Lord, I could barely croak out any words, but I kept at it. Gradually my voice returned, and within a matter of minutes, my body was healed!

Praise God because He is worthy, no matter what you are going through. Even if you feel as if there is no reason to praise God, dare to praise Him for what He has provided for you in the past, and for what He has already provided for you in the future! Remember, you have more to thank God for than you do to complain about.

Even if circumstances aren't going your way, God can turn them around…if you will believe Him. Remember that the act of praising Him is one of the strongest ways you can express your faith. Each time you declare, "Praise God!" you are also saying loud and clear, "I believe God!"

Begin to praise Him right now, right where you are: "Lord, I'm going to praise You." Remind yourself of the three great truths from God's Word: "The LORD is good; His mercy is everlasting, and His truth endures to all generations" (Psalm 100:5). His truth is revealed in His Word, which contains seven thousand promises! Declare right now: "Lord, I thank You that all of Your promises are true, and I believe Your Word today!"

THE LONE LEPER WHO GAVE THANKS

One of the more compelling stories of a thankful person concerns a man healed by Jesus. This is what happened:

> Then as [Jesus] entered a certain village, there met Him ten men who were lepers, who stood afar off. And they lifted up their voices and said, "Jesus, Master, have mercy on us!"
>
> So when He saw them, He said to them, "Go, show your-selves to the priests." And so it was that as they went, they were cleansed.
>
> And one of them, when he saw that he was healed, returned, and with a loud voice glorified God, and fell down on his face at His feet, giving Him thanks. And he was a Samaritan.
>
> So Jesus answered and said, "Were there not ten cleansed? But where are the nine? Were there not any found who returned to give glory to God except this foreigner?" And He said to him, "Arise, go your way. Your faith has made you well." (Luke 17:12–19)

The Bible says, "Rejoice always, pray without ceasing, in everything give thanks; for this is the will of God in Christ Jesus for you" (1 Thessa-lonians 5:16–18). Notice that it does not say to give thanks *for* every-thing. No, the Word commands us to give thanks *in* everything!

You can be squarely in the middle of the worst circumstances of your life and still thank God. Even if you feel as if you are drowning in an impossible situation, keep your eyes on God's promises, His goodness, and His mercy—and then thank Him for all three! Then He can set you free!

This is your day to decide: "I am going to live a life of praise!"

You have more to give thanks about than you do to complain about. Think about this: Are you a complainer, a grumbler, someone who is always looking for the negative? Do you know that negatives are always developed in a darkroom?

Step out of the shadows and into the sunlight of God's Word! Then you will begin to see all the great things God has in store for you. When you praise Him, your whole life opens up to the blessings He wants to rain down upon your life. Become a receptacle of the blessings God wants to pour into you. Make up your mind to develop a rich attitude of gratitude. Declare, "I'm going to be one who gives thanks, rejoices, and is grateful."

When people ask, "How are you doing?" just tell them, "I'm grateful!" When they ask you what you are grateful for, begin to tell them about all of the good things God has done for you. You will discover you have plenty to say on that subject!

Do you see the cup as half empty or half full? Many people say, "Well, I don't have this, and I'm still suffering because of that." They always seem to see the negative in a situation. Then there are others who see the bright side of everything because they see God in the middle of their lives. "I am truly blessed," they say.

When the ten lepers came to Jesus looking for healing, Jesus spoke to them and the healing power of God was released. The Bible says that as they went, they were all cleansed and made whole. Yet only one of those ten lepers turned around and came back to give thanks to Jesus!

That's only 10 percent. Jesus said, "Were there not ten cleansed? But where are the nine?"

Jesus expected all of those who had been healed to return to give thanks, yet only one did. Have you accepted the goodness of God in any form? All of us have! But most of us have also said on a bad day, "Well, what's God done for me lately?"

Are you still breathing? If you are alive, you can give thanks. Everything we have on this planet came from God. When you take a shower or drink a cold glass of water, thank Him for the water you use so freely. Thank Him for sunshine, because the sun is still shining, even when there are clouds. When you begin to think about it, there are so many things that God has done, is doing, and will do for which we should thank Him.

Jesus clearly expected all ten lepers to come back and give Him thanks. He told the one who did return, "Arise, go your way. Your faith has made you well" (Luke 17:19). I find it interesting that all ten lepers were cleansed of leprosy, but only one was made well, or whole, in his spirit, his soul, and his body.

> **D**ecide today and say, "Lord, I'm going to give You thanks every moment of my life."

When you begin to give thanks and become a habitual praiser, rejoicer, and giver of thanks, then you not only receive an answer for your immediate need, but God also makes you whole in every area of your life! This is God's plan and purpose for you! He wants you to move from a daily habit of complaining, griping, and faultfinding to being saturated day and night in continual thanksgiving and rejoicing to the Lord for what He has done.

You make the choice every day. This is more than simply a matter of your personality. Some people say, "Well, I'm just not made that way. That's not really me." The real response is this: it isn't a matter of your personality; it is all about God's personality. I've noticed that even the

grumpiest and most negative people on the planet seem quick to praise a
movie, a sports figure, or a celebrity they like!

An attitude of gratitude may not have been a part of your life in the
past, but things have changed! Make the decision to praise God because
He is worthy. You and I really need to do it because He is good, His Word
is true, and His mercy is everlasting! Decide today and say, "Lord, I'm
going to give You thanks every moment of my life."

"Acie, I Can See! I Can See!"

MAROLYN FORD'S STORY

I'm so thankful that I formed a really close relationship with the Lord
as a young child and continued nourishing that relationship in my
teenage years. He was my Strength and my Friend. I couldn't have
made it without Him.

After high school I was working as a private secretary when one
day, very suddenly, I lost my central vision. I couldn't read or write,
recognize people, drive a car, or see any details around me.

A string of doctors shook their heads, but the last one wrote down
the diagnosis of macular degeneration on my chart. We learned later
this was incorrect, because research has shown that macular degeneration progresses over a twenty-year period. I had gone blind
overnight!

A doctor at the Mayo Clinic told me that I would be blind for the
rest of my life, and I just didn't know how to cope with that.

All of my hopes and dreams of college, career, and marriage
seemed to shatter and fall around me. I didn't know how to pick up
the broken pieces.

I spent the first three weeks of blindness planted in my dad's easy chair. Then I began to listen to the late Ethel Waters as she sang, "His eye is on the sparrow, and I know He watches me."

I listened to this over and over and over again, thinking and praying: *God, You care so much about those little birds. Father, if You take care of them, surely You're going to take care of me.*

Finally, I realized that life is God's gift to us. I also knew that I wouldn't accomplish anything for God by sitting in my dad's chair for the rest of my life. I needed to pick up the broken pieces and pull my life together again.

I typed a letter to the late Dr. Lee Robertson, founder and then-president of Tennessee Temple University, explaining that I was blind but that I wanted to attend the university as a student. I proposed that I record the class lectures and take verbal tests from the instructors.

He wrote back and said, "We've never had a blind student before, but we are willing to give it a try for one semester."

A young man showed me around the campus during my first week at the university. It just so happened that my sister was dating his brother. When I was introduced to this young man, I felt the Lord telling me, *Marolyn, this is the young man that you've been praying for all of these years.*

I thought, *God, I won't tell him. You've got to show it to him, or he will run for sure. Nobody wants to marry a blind girl.*

It turned out that he didn't run, and that man did marry a blind girl! I faced a lot of difficulties getting my college education, and later I also had to take care of the little baby God gave my husband and me. She was a blessing—but the challenges were immense.

I learned to read books in Braille to my daughter that featured a beautiful picture on one side so that she could enjoy the pictures while I read.

Even daily activities can take twice the time when you are blind.

It took me thirty minutes to make sandwiches instead of ten, and I couldn't quickly gather dirty dishes from a dinner table—I had to gently glide my hand over the table to avoid plunging my hand into the middle of some peas or something worse.

When I opened my eyes, I saw my husband right in front of me.

At times I fell into despair, thinking, *God, I just can't keep going like this. Would You please just give me back my eyesight? There's so much that I need to do. God, please, just give sight to my blind eyes.* We prayed earnestly for a miracle for thirteen years.

One night my husband opened the Word of God and read two short verses to me. Then he knelt on his knees in front of me, put his arm over my shoulder, and began to cry out to the Lord: "God, I know You can do it. Father, I know You can give Marolyn back her eyesight. Lord Jesus, when You walked on earth, You healed those who were blind. Lord, I pray that somehow You would restore Marolyn's eyesight tonight."

When I opened my eyes, I saw my husband right in front of me. I said, "Acie, I can see! I can see!"

He said, "What do you mean you can see?"

"Acie, I can see your green eyes and your rosy cheeks and your hair! I can see everything! Acie, I can see! I can see!"

I jumped out of bed and gave him a hug, and then we jumped up and down together. Then I said once again: "Acie, I can see! I can see! I can see everything!"

"Well, can you see the furniture?"

"Yes! I can see the furniture! I can see the beds! I can see the draperies! I can see everything! Acie, this is beautiful! I can see!"

When I ran by the mirror, I got to see what I looked like for the first time in thirteen years. Then I took a second look and I thought, *Oh! A lot of changes have gone on since I was eighteen! Who is that in the mirror?*

Then I rushed out of the room to see my baby for the first time. I can't put into words the joy I experienced when I saw my husband and my daughter for the first time!

That same morning I went straight to my doctor's office for an exam, and I didn't think he'd ever get done examining me. Finally, he stepped back and said: "Marolyn, you walked in here, and you read my letters on the eye exam. It is obvious that you can see. But medically speaking, your eyes have not changed. I don't know what you're seeing with. Honestly, I don't know what to put down on the medical chart. I've never seen anything like this happen."

We serve such a mighty and powerful God. He spoke the world into existence, and He provides everything we need for life. I'm thankful that God healed my eyes. It is such a blessing to be able to see! Now I can't stop singing those words—and supply a few more of my own: "His eye is on the sparrow, and I know—Oh, how I know, my God, the God who created the universe—He watches over me."

UNLEASH THE POWER OF PRAISE

There's an old hymn by Johnson Oatman Jr. that says, "Count your many blessings, name them one by one. And it will surprise you what the Lord hath done." It is true—as you count your blessings, you will see all that God has done. He has done countless wonderful things for you and me. David the psalmist said:

Bless the LORD, O my soul;
>   And all that is within me, bless His holy name!
Bless the LORD, O my soul,
>   And forget not all His benefits:
Who forgives all your iniquities,
>   Who heals all your diseases,
Who redeems your life from destruction. (Psalm 103:1–4)

You and I have so much to give thanks for. Have you been thanking God for His benefits, or have you been pitching fits? Too many people complain when they face bad situations instead of saying, "God, I'm going to thank You in advance for helping me through this struggle. I thank You now instead of later for bringing me through this sickness, taking me through this attack, helping resolve this financial need!"

Begin to give thanks in the middle of what you're going through! Say, "God, I'm going to thank You for who You are, for what You have promised, for what You have done—and for what You are about to do." Then prepare for God to meet you in the middle of your need.

The Bible says God inhabits, is enthroned upon, the praises of those who praise Him (see Psalm 22:3, KJV and NKJV). Praise wounds the Enemy and brings confusion to his ranks. Satan always wanted to be praised in heaven. He wanted the angels to worship him like they worshiped God. He said, "I'm going to be like God. I will exalt myself above the stars. I will be in that place" (see Isaiah 14:13–14). And he was cast down. Jesus said, "I saw Satan fall like lightning from heaven" (Luke 10:18).

When you praise God, you are literally defeating the Enemy because your praise stops the works of darkness! Jesus taught that every time you ask God for something, you need to believe that you have received it (see Mark 11:24). If you truly believe that you have received what you asked for from the Lord, you should give thanks the moment that you pray.

God's people have always praised Him in the midst of their trials. The Israelites once found themselves surrounded by three hostile armies that were threatening to annihilate them. So their leader Jehoshaphat and the people fasted and prayed to God for deliverance. Then God said, "Do not be afraid nor dismayed because of this great multitude, for the battle is not yours, but God's" (2 Chronicles 20:15). So Jehoshaphat sent the praise team out ahead of his soldiers. As God's people began to sing and praise His name, God Himself ambushed the enemy, causing the three armies to turn on one another until they were completely destroyed (see 2 Chronicles 20:18–24)!

If you are in a battle right now and feel surrounded by financial problems on one side, health problems on the other, and family issues in front of you—just do what Jehoshaphat did! Start singing the praises of God from His Word. Sing what the Israelites sang that day: "Praise the LORD, for His mercy endures forever" (2 Chronicles 20:21). I encourage you to praise God, even in the darkest night of your soul! You can praise your way out of it. You have many things to be thankful for.

> God's people have always praised Him in the midst of their trials.

Remember Marolyn Ford's powerful story of how she lived without sight from the age of eighteen until the day thirteen years later when her husband prayed for her and her eyes were opened! Miracles happen when people believe God!

When you pray, remember to praise Him in faith. And when He

answers, remember to be the one who returns to give thanks. Take a moment to pray this prayer of thanksgiving:

Right here and right now, where I am, I praise You, Lord! Thank You for what You have done for me and those I love.

Thank You for providing for my needs, and thank You for sending Your Son to take away my sins, give me a new life, and lead me through to victory in this life and in the life to come!

I praise You for yesterday's blessings, and I praise You for Your provision today. And I praise You now for everything You will do in the days ahead! In Jesus' name, Amen!

12

Pressing On

Life is no cakewalk.

It's a marathon...with plenty of **hurdles**...
    mountains
    valleys
    potholes
    speed bumps
    detours
    ...along the way.

When the race gets **long** and...
    your goals
    your dreams
    your destinations
    ...seem far away...

Keep **your eye** on the prize.
    Don't grow weary.
    Don't lose heart.
    Don't throw in the towel.

When you're feeling winded, God will be your...
  second wind
  third wind
  fourth wind
  fifth wind
  sixth wind

He will **quench** your thirst.

He will **mend** your wounds.

He will be your **strength**.

So...
  go the distance!
  finish strong!
  press on!
  run on!
  keep on keeping on!
  ...until you cross the finish line!

Don't give up.

Don't give up! God has plans for you, but they will take perseverance. You must press on and stay with it! Stay in the game! It's not over till it's over—and it's not over yet!

Jesus is our example. Remember, He is the One who went through all of the suffering, pain, and agony of the cross. He endured rejection and hurt and paid the ultimate price of death to bring us life!

The Bible reveals the key to Jesus' endurance and ability to press on when everything around Him seemed to shout, "Go back, give up, run away, find another way!"

What is this key? Will it work for you? Think about the secret revealed in the book of Hebrews:

> Since we are surrounded by so great a cloud of witnesses, let us lay aside every weight, and the sin which so easily ensnares us, and let us run with endurance the race that is set before us, looking unto Jesus, the author and finisher of our faith, who for the joy that was set before Him endured the cross, despising the shame, and has sat down at the right hand of the throne of God. (12:1–2)

Jesus pressed on because He saw the joy at the end of His race! He was only doing what His Father did! You can probably quote John 3:16, but notice what motivated our heavenly Father to sacrifice the one He loved the most: "For God so loved the world that He gave…" The motivation was love

Jesus fulfilled His Father's deepest desire by willingly laying down His life for you and me. He endured all of the pain because He saw you and me—along with everyone else who received Him as Lord and Savior—saved from darkness, death, and eternal separation from our Father and Creator. Jesus saw Himself taking His rightful position once again at the right hand of the Father as a triumphant, overcoming victor. His anticipation of joy helped Him endure the pain and shame. There was nothing in His passion of tears that He enjoyed or liked, yet He went through it for the joy that was set before Him, in seeing all the lives who would be saved because of His sacrifices.

Right now you may not see any joy in your life, but you can see it ahead. Because of that, you can have joy inside of you as you believe and trust God. The Bible says "the joy of the LORD is your strength" (Nehemiah 8:10)! Peter described this God kind of joy as "joy unspeakable and full of glory" (1 Peter 1:8, KJV). You've got the joy, so no matter what you face, you can persevere and press on until you win the prize!

PATIENCE DOESN'T SURRENDER TO CIRCUMSTANCES!

The Bible urges us to imitate leaders who "through faith and patience inherit the promises" (Hebrews 6:12). God wants you to walk in His promises. Yes, He has promised to fulfill every one of His promises, but you cannot reach "delivery and receipt in full" without patience! That word *patience* means "hanging in there" in rugged circumstances or trials. God promised Abraham that he would father a child by Sarah. It didn't happen for twenty-five years, and that conversation with God took place when Abraham was seventy-five years old! Throughout the next quarter of a century, Abraham was growing in his faith and understanding of God. He learned how to cooperate with God and fulfill the covenant God had made with him. What if Abraham had quit? What if he had surrendered his faith, failed to believe, and let go of it all? We know this much: he wouldn't be honored today as our father in faith.

God had a plan for Abraham, and He has a plan for you too. Don't be surprised if it takes a long time to come to pass.

I remember when I was driving down Lewis Avenue in Tulsa, Oklahoma, in 1982. I looked over at a pecan field and saw with my spiritual eyes a giant white building among those trees.

At the time, we were believing God for a place to build a church building, but I had never thought of this field or of this place until I saw this building in a vision. I pulled into a parking lot across the street from that particular area. (The parking lot just happened to belong to the Mabee Center, a multipurpose arena located on the Oral Roberts University campus.) Then I sketched out a drawing of what I had seen.

It was twenty-five years before what I saw in that vision became a reality—a building that came to be right at that place. During that quarter of a century, we had to battle through seemingly countless challenges and obstacles. We had to go through the sometimes painful process of buying many different pieces of land, and then we felt we were to believe God to go all the way through the building process on a debt-free basis! It was a battle, but it has been worth it! Why? We had a joyful picture in our heart and mind that helped carry us all the way through those years—we did it for the sake of the people whose lives are being transformed today.

You may have a God-given dream, vision, or joy in your heart that looks as if it will never come to pass. Perhaps you have a vision of having a beautiful family or of living your life victoriously. Perhaps you have a dream of overcoming a habit, an addiction, or something else that is a huge struggle in your life. Right now it keeps pressing you down and standing in the way of your miracle. But don't give up the dream. Hold on. Persevere. You will make some sacrifices getting there, but He will reward you. Better days are in store for you!

IF YOU DON'T GET BITTER, YOU'LL MAKE IT!

"Don't give up! Keep pressing on, and one day you will have that breakthrough because you didn't quit, you didn't give up, and you didn't become bitter!"

I heard this helpful advice years ago when I asked a minister, "What one thing can you say to me that will help me in the ministry?" I asked the question as this minister, a guest speaker at a church event, walked across a parking lot to get in his car and leave town. He never even slowed down. He just glanced back at me and said, "If you don't get bitter, you'll make it."

How many people do you know who quit because they got angry, upset, and bitter at other people? My word to you is this: Don't get bitter. Keep pressing on! Here's what pressing on looks like in two key Scripture passages:

Do you not know that in a race all the runners run, but only one gets the prize? Run in such a way as to get the prize. Everyone who competes in the games goes into strict training. They do it to get a crown that will not last; but we do it to get a crown that will last forever. Therefore I do not run like a man running aimlessly. (1 Corinthians 9:24–26, NIV)

> [Instead] let us lay aside every weight, and the sin which so
> easily ensnares us, and let us run with endurance the race that is
> set before us, looking unto Jesus, the author and finisher of our
> faith, who for the joy that was set before Him endured the cross,
> despising the shame, and has sat down at the right hand of the
> throne of God. (Hebrews 12:1–2)

I'm glad that Jesus did not quit on the way to Calvary! He pressed on. He did what the Father had assigned Him to do. Because Jesus refused to quit during His history-changing ordeal about two thousand years ago, today you and I can have eternal life! So I am saying to you, *Don't quit!*

What do you have if you stop? Not much. Remember this: you could be just one push away from a miracle!

Or you can get caught up in reliving past hurts. "Well, those people did this to me and they let me down. You don't understand—they failed me!" It's regrettable, but everybody experiences disappointing and painful things. All of us have been there in one way or another. So what makes you so special in the pain category? Why do you say that you should be able to quit simply because you have suffered pain and loss?

Consider the pain that Jesus suffered. Jesus was rejected. He was innocent and holy, but misinformed and sinful people spat on Him and mocked Him. In fact, His own friends and disciples betrayed Him and ran away. He didn't sit and dwell on it. He kept on going, all the way through to His death on the cross. He did it because He knew that's what God had asked Him to do. He knew that if He did it, then we would have eternal life. Think about it: You need to press on because this isn't just about you. It's also about the lost and hurting people that God has assigned for you to touch and transform!

This is the perfect day to break through any lingering selfishness, discouragement, or depression you're feeling because of past disappointments. Strip off the hindering sense of bitterness, rejection, or abandonment you feel over what you've gone through. Just declare to God—out loud for the world to hear: "Do You know what, Lord? I'm going to forgive. I'm going to forget. I ask for Your forgiveness, and I'm am going on. I will press through with Your help! I will fight through every attack and every battle. Because You are with me, I'm going to win!"

I'm telling you that you are a winner! There is power in the Spirit of God who lives inside of you, and it will raise you up and cause you to be an overcomer.

The book of Hebrews explains your role in all of this: "Let us hold fast the confession of our hope without wavering, for He who promised is faithful" (10:23). Keep on declaring that Word from God out loud: "The same God who put me in this race is going to bring me all the way through to completion! He who began a good work in me is going to complete His work. He is personally working in me to will and to do His good pleasure" (see Philippians 1:6; 2:13)!

Sharon and I have had countless opportunities to quit, but we decided not to. We were determined to keep on pressing on!

Thomas Edison, one of America's greatest inventors, is credited with the invention of the electric light bulb. His success didn't come easily. That man experienced failure (with all of the ridicule, disappointment, and pressure failure produces) more than ten thousand times before he finally experienced the success we remember. What if Edison had quit after the first hundred failures? How about the first two hundred? What if he had decided to move on to another career after failure number three hundred? No, Edison kept saying, "Every wrong attempt discarded is a step forward." He tried to make a light bulb with countless kinds of materials, structures, and methods. Sometimes Edison and his crew made many different attempts in a single day, all because they knew they had a destiny and he had a faithful, dedicated team working with him!

When I was a young boy, I ran my first 440-yard race in a junior high track meet. I remember hearing my dad up in the stands yelling words of encouragement as I prepared for the start of the race. I had to run four laps around the track…and I wasn't very fast. All the while I could hear Dad up in the stands yelling, "Come on, Billy Joe!"

> I heard a voice yelling, "Come on, Billy Joe! Come on, Billy Joe!" The voice sounded close—really close!

When the starter's pistol sounded, all of us tried to start the race at a fast clip. I went around that first curve and headed down the stretch. As I came around the back stretch, I heard a voice yelling, "Come on, Billy Joe! Come on, Billy Joe!" The voice sounded close—really close! When I glanced over my shoulder, I saw my dad! He had left the grandstand while I was running and crossed the field to meet me. He was actually running with me alongside the track!

Now, that can be pretty embarrassing when you're in the seventh grade, but something happened that day that inspired me for the rest of my life. *My dad was running alongside of me, saying, "Come on! Come on! Come on!"*

I don't remember who won our family race that day—Dad or me! But I will never forget *how* we both crossed the finish line.

Long ago Jesus stepped down from the grandstands of heaven to get in the middle of the race with you and me. He is saying to you right now, "Come on! Come on! We can finish this thing!" You can complete what God has assigned you to do. You can break out of that wrong lifestyle that threatens to take your life. You can come out of drug addiction, alcoholism, compulsive gambling, and depression. You can rise above what you lost. You can press through the brokenness you experienced when everything fell apart in your marriage, family, and finances. You can overcome the abuse of your past. You can land that job that God has for you. You can complete that degree in your education process. You can do the work He's assigned you to do.

Don't let go of the things God has said to you. You know He has good plans for you, so don't let go of them just because life is tough. Life is tough on everybody at times. The title of one of Robert Schuller's books says it well: *Tough Times Never Last, But Tough People Do!*

With God's help, you will begin to rise up on the inside and be an overcomer! While other birds and wildlife flee violent storms, the eagle rises above them. When the rest of creation is cowering, running, and seeking shelter, the eagle rises up by setting its face into the brunt of the storm. The very fury of the storm becomes the force that lifts the eagle above the clouds!

Set your face like "flint" (Isaiah 50:7), dare to stare right into the face of your storm, and say, "This wind may be blowing against me, but it is going to lift me higher and higher because I'm getting stronger every day in God's power!"

From Tragedy to Purpose with God's Word

PAM'S STORY

The morning my life changed began like so many others. I got ready for work, said good-bye to my granddaughter, and drove away. But I had no idea that would be the last time I would see my granddaughter alive.

At about eight o'clock that night, my daughter called to frantically tell me that my granddaughter wasn't breathing. Thirty minutes later I arrived at the hospital and rushed in to see her. When I looked in her eyes, I could see no spark of life—her eyes were totally black. I knew at that moment that she would never come back.

I learned later that detectives were already at the hospital investigating the reason for my granddaughter's condition because she was a minor.

My daughter was in the waiting room, and she was hysterical...frantic. When my granddaughter was officially declared dead, the police arrested my daughter and the baby's father right there at the hospital and then took them both to jail. Soon after, my daughter was charged with first-degree murder.

I kept thinking, *This isn't really happening. I'm going to wake up and this is all going to be a dream. This can't possibly be happening to me. I didn't raise my daughter to be a murderer!*

I just keep waiting and hoping that I would wake up and the bad dream would go away. But that's not what happened. At some point it hit me: the nightmare was real.

The funeral was horrific. My daughter wanted to come, but the officials wouldn't allow it. While I was doing my best not to be bitter and angry about my granddaughter's tragic death, my parents came into town from Iowa and focused their anger on me. In their grief, they pointed at me and said, "You are a bad mother. Obviously you did something wrong."

I began to believe it *was* all my fault. I asked myself, *I didn't raise my daughter right... Could I have done something different? Why didn't I do this or that?* When psychiatrists later diagnosed my daughter as being bipolar, I began to ask, *Why didn't I know that? Why didn't I see the warning signs?*

I started retreating to my bedroom. I'd close the window shades, unplug the telephone, lock the door, and crawl into bed. I refused to talk to anyone. My whole world was falling apart.

I'd wake up each morning thinking, *I just want to go somewhere else, anywhere else. I want to get away from this pain and be somebody else—anyone other than who I am. I quit. This is it—I've done enough.*

I went to see a psychiatrist, but by this point I knew she couldn't help me. Finally I told her, "You can't do anything for me. Only God can help me."

She said, "Well, maybe that's true." She went to her bookshelf and pulled out a book entitled *Battlefield of the Mind* by Joyce Meyer. She gave it to me and said, "I think you should read this book."

I took the book, but in the state I was in, I really didn't care about Joyce Meyer, the battle, or anything else. I just wanted to be depressed. So I went home, threw the book on the table, and fell right back into my depression.

> **A**s I cried out and read His Word,
> God kept telling me, *You can't quit.*
> *You've got to stick with it. I am with you!*

Then something happened while I was in bed one day. I heard a voice tell me, *You need to read that book.* So I got up and started reading the book.

Immediately something I read just grabbed hold of me as Joyce Meyer talked about how the devil attacks our mind and how we really have to pay attention if we want to avoid being ensnared by wrong thinking.

What really gripped me were the scriptures she kept quoting throughout the book. I actually had to get up and get my Bible and read the Word as I read the book! To my surprise, it started ministering to me in a way I never expected.

Up until that point I couldn't think or reason clearly. All I could think about were all of the negative things that had happened in my life. Yet even in that confusion I prayed and cried out to God for an answer, and He really answered my prayer!

I am a living testimony that the truth is in the Word, because I know without a doubt that had I continued the way I was going, I would be in a mental institution right now and not sharing my story. As I cried out and read His Word, God kept telling me, *You can't quit. You've got to stick with it. I am with you!*

I thank God every day for my sanity. I also thank Him for my daughter. She was only seventeen years old when all of this happened, and at this writing she has been in prison for almost ten years. God also ministered to her in a powerful way! When I was finally able to go see her, I discovered she was a different person too. Today she ministers to young women in prison!

I know that God has a plan for me and for my daughter. I'm confident that because He is with me, I can walk out His plan every day and be happy. I can go on with my life and press through every challenge in His love.

Because Jesus Christ transformed my pain with His love, I will not allow the pain and sorrow of yesterday to take over my life ever again.

○ ○ ○ ○ ○

DON'T QUIT!

Don't get weary while doing good, for in due season you will reap—if you don't lose heart (see Galatians 6:9)! That is an important word for you from God's heart: *Don't quit!* The good seeds you are planting now are going to grow. At the right time they will yield a great harvest, but it will take time. It is a process.

We live in a time of instant everything, with fast food, express oil changes, and high-speed Internet—everything happens quickly. Many people today struggle to remain steadfast, to persevere, and to endure. If something doesn't happen by the weekend (such as reaching a weight-loss goal or finishing a home-improvement project), then they throw up their hands and say, "Well, I'm out of here!"

Seek to believe and understand that God is working, even when you can't see it. When you plant a seed in the ground today, it isn't going to come up tomorrow! It will take form over a certain period of time, depending on what kind of seed it is. In a similar way, many of the seeds you've planted in your life are still living a hidden life. Nevertheless, the day is coming when they will be visible, when your dreams will be fulfilled.

Declare this right now because this is your time to believe: "God, You are working even when I don't see it. Even when I can't understand it, I refuse to quit just because I haven't seen my harvest yet. I trust You, and I know it is on the way!"

In the Bible, 2 Kings 6:28–29 describes the terrifying day that a powerful army totally surrounded the city of the people of God and put it under siege, blocking all incoming food and water. Things got bad inside the walled city because of both the siege and the sinful lives of the people. In fact, things got so bad that the starving people actually resorted to cannibalism.

Four lepers, who normally were forbidden to enter the city because their disease was considered to be a death sentence to the population, were watching everything happen from outside the city gate. They were in a tough spot, because in better times they survived by scrounging through garbage or receiving gifts of leftover food and clothing from the city's residents. Because of the hard times, though, no one was giving.

The four lepers saw the dire situation. They had a choice of slowly starving outside the walls or of going out to the invading army to beg for food, which might get them killed even quicker!

The four lepers talked about their situation as they sat outside the locked and barred city gate. Here's what they said:

Why are we sitting here until we die? If we say, "We will enter the city," the famine is in the city, and we shall die there. And if we sit here, we die also. Now therefore, come, let us surrender to the army of the Syrians. If they keep us alive, we shall live; and if they kill us, we shall only die. (2 Kings 7:3–4)

As they thought about it, they figured there was a possibility that if they went toward the enemy army, God could do something amazing. So just after the sun slipped below the horizon, the four lepers started dragging their crippled and bandaged bodies down the road leading to the enemy camp. Next came the miracle! God caused their scraping feet, dragging on that ancient road, to sound like a massive army of thundering chariots and war-horses! When the invading army heard those sounds, they became so frightened that they ran out of their camp in absolute terror! They totally abandoned all of their tents, supplies, gold and silver, and even all their clothes (see 2 Kings 7:7–8)! Their food was still cooking on their campfires!

In one night, these four forsaken lepers and outcasts went from the point of starvation and death to possessing more than enough to feed all the starving people inside the city walls.

> "I refuse to quit just because I haven't seen my harvest yet. I trust You, and I know it is on the way!"

Right this moment you may be looking at your circumstances and saying, "I'm going to starve here. I don't see how anything good can come of this." But I want you to ask yourself these questions: *What if I do the thing that God told me to do? What if I just step out and obey Him—even if I have to drag myself to that point?*

What might happen if you don't quit? If you don't give up, you might discover you've made that one last push to produce the miracle God has for you!

Remember, it wasn't easy for Jesus to carry that cross up Calvary's hill, but He did it for you. It wasn't easy to go through the rejection, the mocking, and all of the suffering He endured. It wasn't easy, as an innocent man, to die for the guilty. But Jesus persevered because He loves you.

Don't let any trouble, problem, or difficulty dictate the direction of your life. Go back to what God said to you on the inside!

It is time for you to depend upon the Holy Spirit who lives inside of you. Say, "Lord, help me not to quit. Help me not to throw in the towel. Help me to stay with it and run all the way through the race that You have assigned to me."

Lay aside every weight and sin. Run with patience, perseverance, steadfastness, and endurance. Finish the race that God has set before you. Complete your assignment in this life. Do the job God called you to do, whether it is to bring hope and unity to your family, stability to your home, or salvation to people who have never experienced the love of Jesus.

13

The Promise
of Eternity

Are you living for **eternity**?
    Your life is but a vapor...
    a brief moment...
    a dash between two dates...your birth-death.

Are you making the most of your dash?

Instead of **living for** the mansion...
    the sports car
    the sailboat
    the toys

...why not live for something more?

Why not **spend** more of...
    your time
    your money
    your life

your **dash**
   mending wounds
   building bridges
   sharing your stuff
   listening
   encouraging
   loving others as God loves you?

Life is short.

Eternity is long.

You only get **one chance**...
   one shot
   one dash

So why not **make yours count** for eternity?

ternity is forever. If that is true, then what are you living for? *Why* are you living? Do you realize that what you do today, right here and now, directly affects what happens in eternity?

The Bible says that *everything that we do* will be revealed at the judgment seat of Christ (see Romans 14:10 and 2 Corinthians 5:10). Some of the things we've done will pass the test and shine like valuable gold, silver, and precious stones. Many of the other things we've done won't make it through the fire of God's presence. They will go up in smoke, like wood, hay, and stubble, because they have no substance or value before Him who *is* eternity. They'll be burned and gone forever (see 1 Corinthians 3:11–15).

Imagine someone with the ability to help thousands of people. Now imagine that in order to win some meaningless contest, this person instead spends his whole life building the world's largest house out of wooden matchsticks. After decades of total focus on a pile of sticks, someone comes along and thoughtlessly strikes one match. In minutes, this man's lifework goes up in flames, leaving behind nothing but ashes...*and a life-*

time wasted. His life didn't count for anything. It was basically *a life lived for zero.*

The truth is that most of us devote most of our time and energy to accomplishing things that are worth little more than matchsticks! How many millions of Americans work diligently for decades hoping to attain the American dream so they can walk away with a gold watch and spend their remaining years in a fishing boat or traveling?

The sad truth is that Fortune 500 companies have begun to fall like so many matchsticks in our ever-changing world. Millions reach retirement age only to find their company has declared bankruptcy or that their retirement fund has faded away, along with their future. Many younger people revolt against that stereotype, but they have little more to look forward to.

I have very good news for you! You have the opportunity to *make a difference* with your life! You can decide to live your life for God and accomplish things that He calls "gold, silver, [and] precious stones" (1 Corinthians 3:12). I'm talking about what happens *after* you surrender your life to Jesus Christ, as important as that is. This is the part of your life Jesus described when He said, "If anyone desires to come after Me, let him deny himself, and take up his cross daily, and follow Me" (Luke 9:23).

Most of the time, it seems that people spend their lives doing only what *they* think is important. Here's the problem: our thoughts about what really matters aren't worth a pile of matches. God said this about our thoughts compared to His:

"For My thoughts are not your thoughts,
   Nor are your ways My ways," says the LORD.
"For as the heavens are higher than the earth,
   So are My ways higher than your ways,
   And My thoughts than your thoughts." (Isaiah 55:8–9)

Living a Life That Counts

The only way to develop a clear understanding of what is valuable, treasured, and eternal in God's view is to go to His Word. That is the only authorized source for learning how to live a life that will count forever!

The Bible reveals powerful principles that show how every prayer you pray in love and faith, especially those prayed for others, and every kind word or deed that you've done are etched in the unfailing memory of God! One reason God's Word is our unfailing source on the promise of eternity is because the Word of God itself is *eternal.* On the other hand, the Bible also says that *all flesh,* which includes you and me, is like grass:

> All flesh is as grass,
> And all the glory of man as the flower of the grass.
> The grass withers,
> And its flower falls away,
> *But the word of the LORD endures forever.*
>   (1 Peter 1:24–25, emphasis added)

Think about the contrast between Moses and Pharaoh in the Bible. Moses was an Israelite, a male baby who had been rescued from the waters of the Nile River by Pharaoh's daughter. It really was a rescue in the sense that Pharaoh, fearing the rapid growth of the Israelite slave population, had ordered that all male babies born to the Hebrews be killed. Yet to God it wasn't an accident but a part of God's divine plan.

Pharaoh's daughter named the baby *Moshe,* which means "drawn out" of the water. She adopted him as her own son, which gave him full rights and privileges as a prince of Egypt (again by divine design). Since Moses was raised by Pharaoh's daughter in the royal palace, he could have ascended to the throne and position of Pharaoh. Instead Moses made a hard choice that is similar to the choice you and I must make today. Scripture says that Moses

> refused to be called the son of Pharaoh's daughter, choosing rather
> to suffer affliction with the people of God than to enjoy the pass-
> ing pleasures of sin, esteeming the reproach of Christ greater riches
> than the treasures in Egypt; *for he looked to the reward.* By faith he
> forsook Egypt, not fearing the wrath of the king; for *he endured as
> seeing Him who is invisible.* (Hebrews 11:24–27, emphasis added)

Sharon and I once visited the Egyptian museum where we saw the vast stores of gold, the ornate carriages, and all of the priceless earthly and archaeological treasures preserved from one of the great civilizations in human history. Moses turned and walked away from all of that *because he chose God*! He saw by faith the day that Christ would come.

When you make the decision to follow Jesus, know that everything you do will be etched in God's book and remembered forever.

Jesus once encountered a young man who wanted to follow Him but needed to make a critical decision. Here's how the story unfolded:

> Now as [Jesus] was going out on the road, one came running,
> knelt before Him, and asked Him, "Good Teacher, what shall
> I do that I may inherit eternal life?"
>
> So Jesus said to him, "…You know the commandments.…"
>
> And he answered and said to Him, "Teacher, all these things
> I have kept from my youth."
>
> Then Jesus, looking at him, loved him, and said to him,
> "One thing you lack: Go your way, sell whatever you have and
> give to the poor, and you will have treasure in heaven; and come,
> take up the cross, and follow Me."

But he was sad at this word, and went away sorrowful, for he had great possessions. (Mark 10:17–22)

This young man determined that the treasures of earth were of more value to him than the treasures of heaven. Did he understand that eternity is forever? Do you? Are you preparing for it? Some people make elaborate preparations for their funeral. They carefully preselect what clothing should be put on their body in the casket and outline every detail of what will happen in the memorial service. Yet, despite all of those preparations, once the service is over, *it's over,* and those in attendance go on with their lives.

Even if you were to add together every day of our earthly existence *plus* the funeral that follows, it all is still only a very brief time in comparison to eternity.

One experience I had involving eternity literally transformed my life. Many years ago I was standing on a football practice field and had a vision in which I saw millions of people living for one thing after another. Some spent their time and money to get an education or land a job. Others focused their hopes on getting married and having a family. But they all seemed determined to get a newer car, buy a larger house, get new furniture—to add more to their pile of possessions. They raced through their life at breakneck speed to get to the place where they could retire, get a house on the lake, buy a boat, and die.

At the end of the vision, I saw a flash and heard God say these words: "Nothing they have done will go into eternity."

I'll never forget standing there in full football gear with my helmet on, with tears flooding my eyes. In that moment, I realized these folks were people that I knew in my hometown! They had lived all their lives for things they thought were important and special. Yet, in the end, nothing they had done was done for God. None of those plans, accomplishments, possessions, or pursuits had been done for His honor and glory. So, at the end of their lives, it was over. Everything was gone.

Then I heard God say, *You can make a decision to live for Me, to go where I tell you to go and do what I tell you to do.*

I was stunned. I had never thought about my life that way. It was a divine revelation given to me by the Spirit of God. It wasn't a revelation that I would never get an education: I was privileged to earn bachelor's and master's degrees and even to earn a doctorate. God wasn't telling me I would never have a wife and family: God brought Sharon and me together, and He gave us four wonderful children and two grandchildren (at this writing). We have been blessed beyond measure!

> **L**ife is about what we do on this earth for God and how we touch people with His love.

God wasn't saying that I would never have a house or a vehicle. God has provided all of those things, as they were needed. He was teaching me the truth of Jesus' words in Matthew 6:33: "Seek ye first the kingdom of God, and his righteousness; and all these things shall be added unto you" (KJV). He revealed the most important thing I could do for eternity: *live my life for God.* I realized it wasn't just about becoming a preacher. He wanted me first and above all to be *someone who followed God.* That is something *anyone* and *everyone* can do! The Lord said:

Will you surrender your life to Me—to go where I tell you to go and do what I tell you to do?

Then when you come to the end of your life, you won't look back on things that you've gained, money that you've earned, or houses and cars that you've had. None of that is going to mean anything.

You will look back on the people your life has touched, and they will all go into eternity to be with Me.

That vision changed the course of my life! When I realized what eternity was all about, it altered everything. *Life is about what we do on this earth for God and how we touch people with His love.* It doesn't matter whether you are a mechanic, a hotel manager, a small-business owner, or if you work at home. You can touch people with God's love wherever you are.

When I went to God in prayer about the words spoken to me, He said they weren't just for me; they were for others too. *That means they are for you too!*

You can make a decision to live for God and live a life without regret. The Lord said to me, *Tell this story to other people,* so I am obeying His command once again as you read these words.

One time I related this story in a meeting, and an older gentleman came up to me in tears and said, "I'm the guy you were talking about in that vision."

"What do you mean?" I asked, and he answered, "I am retired, I live on a lake, and we're out there just waiting to die. I've spent my whole life living for things."

The good part of this story is that as we talked he made a decision to give his life for God, and he spent the rest of his years helping people. This man and his wife started a little prayer group in their home, and bikers (the type of bikers who own choppers and ride in gangs) started coming to the meetings. This couple began to share Jesus with them, and now they've touched many people in their latter years. Today Arlis and Virginia Cole would tell you they touch people *because they made a decision to live for God.* And I am telling you that *it is never too late*!

The Night Our Family Survived a Trial by Fire

SHARON DAUGHERTY'S STORY

Life is a vapor. It's fleeting and passes quickly. All of us will face eternity one day.

One night during the month of October in 1991, we were having our family devotions, with each of the children praying in turn. Ruthie, who was eleven at the time, prayed, "Thank You, Lord, that we shall live and not die to declare the wonderful works of the Lord," which is based on a passage from Psalm 118.

I remember thinking at the time, *That was an unusual scripture—I've never heard Ruthie pray that before.*

We agreed with her prayer by adding together, "In Jesus' name, we agree." Of course none of us even remotely suspected that we might face a life-or-death crisis that night.

We got the children all tucked into bed and I thought, *Well, I'll go through the house to make sure lights are turned off, doors are locked, and everything is ready so that we can go to sleep.* Once I completed my rounds, I went to bed.

At about two o'clock in the morning, I was suddenly awakened out of my sleep. I heard my husband, Billy Joe, scream, "The house is on fire! We've got to get out *now*. Everybody get out!"

I leaped up out of bed at about the same time that our daughter Sarah leaped up. Billy Joe said, "You go into the rooms and get the children out, and I'll run to the front door to try to get it open."

I quickly ran into the room where our sons, John and Paul, were sleeping and began to shake them and say, "Boys, we've got to get out! The house is on fire!"

I thought they were right behind me, so I ran into Ruthie's room and shook her and once again said, "Ruthie, get up. We've got to get out! The house is on fire!"

When I felt sure she was up, I turned back again to the hallway, where I was sure I could feel Sarah, my older daughter, right behind me and almost touching me. I also felt like there was somebody behind her.

The problem was all of this took place in smoky, pitch-black conditions in the dead of night. I couldn't see my hand in front of my face! To make matters worse, everything around us was hot. We could feel the intensity of the heat, but we didn't know where the fire was located in the house.

We started running down the hallway, feeling our way in the blackness and anticipating the final turn toward the front door. When we got there, we found my husband wrestling with the jammed lock on the front door. He finally got the mechanism unlatched, but it had cost him dearly—the metal was so hot that it had severely burned his hands.

And as we ran out, we were all coughing and gasping for air. That is when Billy Joe shouted, "Is everybody out here?" All I could think of was, *I didn't feel Ruthie!* So I said, "No, Ruthie's still inside!"

As I fought off the dread, I could hear Ruthie's small voice coming from the interior of the house. She was crying, "Mommy, Daddy! Mommy, Daddy!" And again I said, "Ruthie's still in there!"

Billy Joe went back in through the front door and felt his way through the smoke and darkness in the hallway. When he reached Ruthie's room, he felt the top of her head and instantly grabbed her by the hair (it was the most available "handle" at the moment).

Knowing every minute was precious, Billy Joe pulled Ruthie down the hallway until they were both out of the house and in the cool night air. He was coughing and fighting to catch his breath when I realized that our son Paul was still in our darkened house with the heat and smoke.

> "**D**addy, I did what the fireman said,
> and I knew that you were going
> to come back in for me."

Between his gasps for air and uncontrollable coughs, Billy Joe had barely escaped the front door with Ruthie before he asked all of us once again, "Do we have everybody?" And again I said, "No. Paul...Paul is still in there!"

For the second time, Billy Joe took a deep breath and began staggering back toward the front door. I was thinking, *He's about to fall over.* I was concerned because he had inhaled so much smoke, and he was weaving and unsteady on his feet.

He looked at me and said, "I'm going back in." Then he vanished again through the front door.

Praise the Lord, Billy Joe found Paul on the floor in the hallway, just waiting. We learned later that Paul's kindergarten teacher had invited a fireman to speak to the class on the day of the fire. The fireman had told the students, "If you are ever in a fire inside a building, you need to get down low and crawl to get out."

Later on, Paul said, "Daddy, I did what the fireman said, and I knew that you were going to come back in for me."

After Billy Joe came out with Paul, we all ran to move away from the house. We gathered ourselves and started to cross the street to our neighbor's house. Just after we had moved away from the house, all of the windows in the house exploded outward. I saw fire licking downward along the entire front of the house. The fire seemed to converge on the ground, right where we had been standing just moments earlier!

As we stood outside, watching the flames devour the place we called home, this thought came to me: *Life is more precious and more important than anything, including all of our stuff and material possessions.*

I was so thankful that we were all alive and standing there together. I wasn't thinking before it all happened, *We are going to have a fire that will burn down our house and consume much of what we own.* But it did, and I had no regrets. My family is more important than anything!

Today, those children, who were just six, seven, eleven, and thirteen the night the fire broke out, are adults—*and are reaching people for Christ.* I know God spared our lives that night so that all of us could fulfill His purpose here on earth, so our lives would mean something and stand for something. We lived through that trial by fire so that we could help other people get ready to face eternity.

○ ○ ○ ○ ○

LIVING ON EARTH, LIVING FOR HEAVEN

We will never forget that night when our family went through the fire. I remember the sinking feeling that hit me when part of our family made it out of the house, and Sharon suddenly said, *"Where's Ruthie?"* And then it was, *"Where's Paul?"* I remember how we screamed out their names and realized they were still inside the house. I vividly recall how I felt the moment I knew I had to go back down that dark hallway through the searing heat and fumes. I still remember the emotions I felt when my hand touched Ruthie's hair in the smoky darkness where she had been waiting for help. When I think about how I pulled her out down that hallway and through the door, I know it was a miracle.

We thank God that we didn't lose our lives simply because of the superheated air and fumes we were breathing. As many people perish because of the fumes in house fires as those who die because of the flames or collapsing structures.

Once I got back outside with Ruthie, I had breathed in so much of the fumes and heat that I was staggering. And it was in that moment that Sharon said, *"Paul is still in there!"* He was our little six year old, and I was determined to get him out.

Determined or not, I was in great pain as I turned back toward the burning house. My hands were badly burned, and I struggled to get my breath, but I *had to do something* to save my son. Praise God, we got him out. Paul had waited, firmly believing he would be rescued—and he was.

Once we were safely across the street, we sat together on our neighbor's front porch and hugged each other. Then we began to praise God for keeping us alive.

It didn't matter to us that everything we owned was burning up and six fire trucks plus rescue squads were on our street trying to put out the fire. We were alive and together.

As we talked with the firemen, it became clear the type of miracle we had experienced. They shook their heads and told us, "Hardly anyone escapes a fire like that one." They couldn't believe that we all got out, because the fire had really taken hold between one and two o'clock in the morning when everybody was sound asleep. That is especially dangerous, because a house fire tends to be so quiet early on as the smoke fills up every space inside a home. (The fire occurred before smoke detectors were commonly installed in homes.)

It's clear that we survived only through *a miracle* from heaven! It made us think about what really counts. Too many of us are like the rich young man who didn't follow Jesus, because he valued and treasured his money and possessions more than he valued the pursuit of God. It is vitally important that you evaluate what really counts the most in your life. What is going to remain here as a testimony to your existence *after* you die?

Eternity is forever.

Your life here on this planet is just like *one grain of sand* compared to eternity, which is like *all of the sand* on all the seashores of the world. If you keep that foremost in your mind, it will help you make wiser decisions and live with eternity in mind.

It is amazing to me that so many people don't realize that *eternity is for everyone.* Whether they believe it or not, everybody is going to exist eternally. That choice isn't theirs to make. However, God gives everyone the choice to spend eternity *with Jesus in heaven.*

I've found that once people understand that truth, then they realize how important it is to make that *most important of all decisions* immediately, and live accordingly! Once that decision is made, it becomes natural to live on purpose with the promise of eternity in mind.

I made that decision long ago, and I've lived as if my life were not my own—because it isn't. I've been "bought at a price" (see 1 Corinthians 7:23). I belong to God alone. My goal is to touch as many lives with the love of Jesus as I can in my brief journey here. Then I can welcome an incredible company of friends into the Lord's presence in eternity!

That is how you live the 360-degree life—knowing that you started with God, entered the world, touched others during your brief stay, and finally completed the circle to enter eternity with God! As the Bible says, "In Him we live and move and have our being" (Acts 17:28).

That's the 360-degree life!

Epilogue

A Personal Note from
Sharon Daugherty and the Family
December 2009

On Sunday, November 22, 2009, my husband, Pastor Billy Joe Daugherty, left this earth and went to heaven at about 4:40 a.m., with the family gathered around his bed at the M. D. Anderson Cancer Center in Houston, Texas.

This book was in its final editing stages when Billy Joe went to be with the Lord. The content in these pages, and the television series it is based on, represent a genuine 360-degree view of his life and ministry in Jesus Christ.

Some have said these two words seem to best describe Billy Joe— *humility* and *integrity.* I personally know that he had a servant heart. His motive in ministry and in building was to further the kingdom of God and to bring God honor. His only goal was to glorify God.

This book was the final project of my husband's lifelong ministry. It will remain as a lasting testimony, challenge, and source of encouragement for the untold thousands of people who will read these words or view the thirteen-segment television series. The sole purpose behind their creation was to help people "seek first the kingdom of God and His righteousness" (Matthew 6:33) and live transformed lives as living witnesses for Christ.

Billy Joe and I were both saved and called by God in 1970. Billy Joe had visions from God before either he or I knew anything about the supernatural. His first vision came after we had returned from a youth trip. He was riding in the backseat of his parent's car as they drove through the night to go see one of his brothers in the military. In this vision he saw the two of us ministering together to masses of people. Although we had no teaching on the supernatural at that point in our lives, he knew from that vision that we would be married. Later, Billy Joe received the vision we shared in chapter 13, "The Promise of Eternity," which deeply impacted the direction of our lives. God said to Billy Joe:

> *Will you surrender your life to Me—to go where I tell you to go and do what I tell you to do?*
>
> *Then when you come to the end of your life, you won't look back on things that you've gained, money that you've earned, or houses and cars that you've had. None of that is going to mean anything.*
>
> *You will look back on the people your life has touched, and they will all go into eternity to be with Me.*

God told Billy Joe that it was not just about becoming a preacher—this was His divine will for every person, regardless of occupation or natural inclination. He wants each of us to touch people with God's love and lead them to Jesus Christ, and He needs each of us in every arena of life.

After this vision, all Billy Joe thought about was how he could touch the lives of people and how he could reach a greater harvest of souls for God's kingdom.

Charles H. Spurgeon once said that Jesus "sees, in every sinner, the possibility of making a glorified saint, who shall dwell with him for ever and ever." My husband seemed to see that same heavenly potential in everyone he met! Whether on the mission field or in our nation's capital,

Billy Joe made it a point to connect with people from all walks of life. He had a way of making people feel comfortable and accepted.

Life itself was a mission field for Billy Joe, but foreign missions were very special to him. He simply loved people of all walks of life and openly shared the love of God wherever he went in his travels, whether he was at a local gas station filling his tank or in Pakistan, the Dominican Republic, or the former Soviet Union.

He would go to any length to share the love of Jesus. When the former Soviet Union opened to the gospel in 1990, Billy Joe traveled once a month for eighteen months to minister the gospel of salvation to a hurting nation. Today, multitudes of children know the name of Billy Joe Daugherty and remember him as one of the key people God used to bring salvation through Jesus to the former Communist country.

Billy Joe entered eternity in November 2009, but only after waging a vigorous fight of faith with lymphoma. He was a man who preached the gospel of Jesus Christ without compromise, and he believed that God still heals and works miracles today. Many people around the world experienced healing and miraculous deliverance through the work of the Holy Spirit as my husband prayed for the sick in Jesus' name.

We are always conscious of the fact that believers watch their leaders to see how they react in times of crisis and adversity. Billy Joe faced adversity throughout his lifetime, and he always put his absolute trust in God. He did the same thing in his own personal battle with illness. It may strengthen your own faith if you know some of the key events that led to my husband's move to heaven.

A HEALTH ISSUE—NOVEMBER 1988

Billy Joe was quite an athlete, and over the years he and I often jogged together for exercise. He was a hard-working person, and he often pushed himself to accomplish ministry projects. Throughout our lives together, Billy Joe spent many hours teaching, training, leading, reconciling, connecting, and helping people get saved.

In November 1988, Billy Joe began to feel extremely tired and weak. He was admitted to City of Faith Hospital in Tulsa and was diagnosed with chronic lymphocytic leukemia (CLL). Doctors knew very little about this rare disease, and no cure or effective treatment was available at the time.

On the third day in the hospital, Billy Joe felt the presence of God in his room as the Lord touched his body, and he felt as if God had healed him. After resting and regaining his strength, Billy Joe pressed ahead with outreaches that increased our ability to reach the harvest in our city, across the nation, and around the world.

A HEALTH CHALLENGE—TWENTY-ONE YEARS LATER

In the summer of 2008, we were headed to Rwanda, Africa, for a crusade and some leadership meetings and conferences. Any airplane flight to south and central Africa can be an endurance contest because of the vast distances and long flight times required to make the trip. By the time we arrived in Rwanda on this trip, Billy Joe was red with fever. The right side of his neck was swollen, and he was extremely tired. He rested during the daytime hours for two days and limited his activity to teaching one daytime leadership session. Each night, however, Billy Joe preached to large crowds of people gathered in a sports field.

Once we returned to Tulsa, he met with our family doctor who referred him to a specialist. The specialist happened to be the same doctor who had diagnosed him in 1989. He received medical care here in Tulsa, and last June it appeared that he had overcome the illness and was feeling well. The specialist was very encouraging because of medical advances that now allowed doctors to treat this disease effectively. However, he felt that at some point Billy Joe should be checked at M. D. Anderson because of their specialization with this particular disease.

During our annual Word Explosion in August 2009, Billy Joe's glands on the right side of his neck began to swell. When Billy Joe returned to the specialist in Tulsa, he was concerned about the glands and referred my husband immediately to M. D. Anderson Cancer Center in Houston. After our consultation there, we returned to Tulsa with an appointment to return to M. D. Anderson in another month.

When he developed a sore throat and other complications, he was hospitalized locally and diagnosed with lymphoma. We alerted our congregation, friends, and prayer partners to pray intensely. We returned to M. D. Anderson Cancer Center for treatment, and then flew back to Tulsa from Houston to perform our son Paul's wedding on October 17.

At first it appeared the cancer cells were dying and new bone marrow was being produced. However, another infection set in and other cancer cells appeared in another part of his body as Billy Joe weakened physically.

In November we returned to M. D. Anderson Cancer Center. People all over the earth were praying around the clock, and we thank God for their wonderful prayer support during this difficult time.

Early on Sunday morning, November 22, Billy Joe left this earth and went to heaven. I felt I was to pray for physical resurrection, but sometime after three hours of prayer, I began to worship and heard the voices of angels singing with me. When I looked down, Billy Joe had a smile on his face that remained.

Pressing Forward to Reach the Harvest

When we returned home after Billy Joe's passing, we found a notepad on his desk, and on it he had scribbled John 4:35, where Jesus said, "Do you not say, 'There are still four months and then comes the harvest'? Behold, I say to you, lift up your eyes and look at the fields, for they are already white for harvest!"

On the morning when Billy Joe passed into heaven, our family was gathered around his bed. My son, Paul, said, "Mom, we are the farm family! Remember Dad's favorite DVD, *The Harvest*?" This short film is about a family who farms. The father passes away in the middle of harvest time, but God sends other farmers to help bring in the harvest. We believe we are harvesters, and there's a call from heaven rallying Christians to continue what Billy Joe saw in his heart—masses of people being reached in these last days. Together we can reach this world.

Billy Joe's memorial service was held on Monday, November 30, 2009, and it was all about the harvest and how God needs all of us to reach this world. When our friend, John Bevere, closed his address during the service, he compared Billy Joe's life to a seed planted in the ground. He said Billy Joe's life does not end with him, that the call he carried will go on through all of us who choose to let God use our lives in this hour.

We are determined to keep our focus on Jesus and go after the harvest with a new intensity.

Another remarkable thing happened when we returned home. We found the manuscript of a booklet Billy Joe had placed on our kitchen counter called *Victory Over Death*. It has now been published. After a lifetime spent building up, encouraging, and comforting others, it amazes me that Billy Joe somehow managed to comfort those of us in his own family after his death! He wrote a prayer in the back of the booklet to help families trying to grapple with living without a loved one. It reveals the depths of his heart and the nature of Billy Joe's God-given gift to lift up others. We've reproduced the prayer here in its entirety, and we pray that it will be a source of joy and strength for you through the Holy Spirit, just as it was for us:

Father, we cover this family with Your grace and mercy in the name of Jesus Christ of Nazareth.

From this hour, I pray that You would give grace, strength, help, and mercy to each surviving family member. Surround them day and night, Lord, with songs of deliverance and peace. May they hear words of Scripture coming back to them—Your promises that never fail.

In the name of Jesus, we bless them and we raise our shields of faith around them.

We say, no fiery dart of the wicked one will touch, harass, or torment their lives, but they will go from glory to glory and from strength to strength.

Thank You, Father, that You will restore, heal, and make each one whole. Thank You that they will comfort and bless others with the comfort and blessing they receive from You.

Ministry will flow through them continually as part of their healing and for the healing of others. In the mighty name of Jesus we pray and we agree. Amen.

We have found ourselves walking out Billy Joe's prayer as ministry flows through us continually as part of our healing and for the healing of others in the mighty name of Jesus! We sensed an unusually strong anointing from the Lord as we participated in Billy Joe's home-going service.

My husband received many honors in his lifetime, but he wore them loosely because there was really only one honor he really desired above all others: to hear these words, "Well done, good and faithful servant.… Enter into the joy of your lord" (Matthew 25:23). Now he has!

We have accepted Billy Joe's baton of reaching the harvest and finishing our race set before us. He made his life count, and his example inspires us to make our lives count as well. So we refuse to become stuck in a place of questioning and doubt or self-focused thinking. We choose to see the fields that are white for harvest.

Hurting and lost people are waiting for the good news of God's love in Jesus Christ! Join us as we complete the 360-degree journey from glory to glory, looking to Jesus and extending His hand to the hurting and the lost!

Sharon

Sarah, Caleb, Isaac, and Elizabeth

Ruth and Adam

John

Paul and Ashley

WITHDRAWAL